A YEAR OF
LIVING MINDFULLY

A YEAR of LIVING MINDFULLY

WEEK-BY-WEEK MINDFULNESS MEDITATIONS FOR A MORE CONTENTED AND FULFILLED LIFE

ANNA BLACK

CICO BOOKS
LONDON NEW YORK

Published in 2015 by CICO Books
An imprint of Ryland Peters & Small Ltd

20–21 Jockey's Fields   341 E 116th St
London   New York
WC1R 4BW   NY 10029

www.rylandpeters.com

10 9 8 7 6 5 4 3 2 1

Text © Anna Black 2015
Design and illustrations © CICO Books 2015

A CIP catalog record for this book is
available from the Library of Congress
and the British Library.

ISBN: 978 1 78249 302 0

Printed in China

Editor Rosie Lewis
Designer Sarah Rock
Illustrator Amy Louise Evans

In-house editor Dawn Bates
In-house designer Fahema Khanam
Art director Sally Powell
Production manager Gordana Simakovic
Publishing manager Penny Craig
Publisher Cindy Richards

CONTENTS

PRACTICES

ACTIVITIES

Starting with the **Week 1 activity on page 12,**
gradually build up your practice **over 52 weeks**
combining it with meditations from the list of practices.

REFLECT ...

Use the note pages throughout the book to
reflect on your experience and learning
in any way you would like to.

INTRODUCTION

The quality of mindfulness is inherent in each of us, but most of us need a little help to cultivate and strengthen it. *A Year of Living Mindfully* is an opportunity to do just that— to introduce and integrate mindfulness into our everyday lives.

When we are mindful, we pay attention to our experience as it unfolds, and we do that in a very particular way: without judging it. It is incredibly simple in itself, but extraordinarily difficult to remember! This book is designed to support your practice, thereby making it easier to remember to do it. Included throughout are topics to motivate you, such as *The Benefits of Present Moment Awareness* (see page 48) and *Stress and How It Affects Us* (see page 92), as well as answers to the question *What Is Mindfulness?* (see page 10), suggestions on *How Best to Support Your Practice* (see page 62), and other themes.

Each week introduces a different activity for you to experiment with. Some are informal practices—that is, doing something you would be doing anyway, but in a different way— but it is also helpful to set aside time to be with yourself and your experience as it arises. This is what is called "formal" meditation. Both types are important.

When we "sit" in formal meditation we are practicing being with different states of mind— boredom, restlessness, agitation, sleepiness, and so on—as well as pins and needles, an aching back, or an itch on the end of our nose. We notice how we resist and push away the experiences we don't like, and we try to hold on to the periods of calm. We practice being with all these different experiences while in a safe environment, so that we can take these skills and apply them to difficulties that may arise in the "outside" world.

Build up your meditation practice gradually. It is better to do a little every day than an hour or so sporadically. Be realistic about what you can make time for. Begin with *Watching the Breath* (see page 26) for 5 or 10 minutes, and build on that. The meditation practices are given in a particular order. It is helpful to begin with body-focused practices, such as *Watching the Breath, Mindfulness of Breath and Body* (see page 70), and *Mindful Movement* (see page 40). Once you have become used to meditating, you can experiment with longer practices, such as *Being With Sounds and Thoughts* (see page 102), *Being With the Difficult* (see page 128), *Self-compassion* (see page 144), and *The Mountain* (see page 156). *The Breathing Space* (see

page 88) and *Mindful Eating* (see page 56) are a bridge between formal and informal practices and can be done from the start.

Practice means doing something over and over again. Through it, we learn to be patient and let go of expectation. We can't order ourselves to be "more patient" or "more accepting," but these qualities can arise if we repeatedly respond differently to our experience. The beauty of setting an intention to practice over an entire year is that there will be plenty of opportunity to see how our practice changes over time—waxing and waning—as well as to experience its benefits.

It is important to remember that mindfulness is not a miracle cure that will magic your stress and other problems away. It isn't, and it won't. However, if you practice regularly you will learn to respond rather than react automatically to what you don't like. Whether the discomfort is physical or psychological, with mindfulness we practice turning toward it with a sense of friendly curiosity, rather than avoiding it or shutting it out. Every time we do this we strengthen the response and approach mode rather than the react and avoid mode that will cultivate our fight or flight response (see page 93). The "pause" that allows us to respond to a difficult moment in everyday life arises naturally from practicing regularly in this way.

It is important to acknowledge that no one can be happy all the time. It is perfectly normal to feel sadness and other difficult emotions from time to time. Experiencing disappointment, pain, illness, grief, and loss is part of being human. However, we can strengthen our resilience to enable us to move through periods of suffering rather than get stuck in them.

While there are clearly benefits to being in constant contact with the world, modern technology can also make us always alert to what might come up—that email or text, a breaking news story, or some Facebook drama. If we are living with a subconscious undercurrent of hypervigilance, the body is under constant stress (see page 92). We are also rarely on our own, and so we may become uncomfortable with being alone with our thoughts and feelings.

Mindfulness helps us learn to surf the waves of life rather than let ourselves be swept away by them. We may still feel emotions strongly—perhaps even more than before, since our present moment awareness may be more acute than the average person's—but we recover from them more quickly and the mind and body return to equilibrium much faster.

Gradually we can introduce behavior and activities into our daily life that nourish us mentally as well as physically. When we are interested in an activity, we may move into a mental state of "flow," which is characterized by calm and focus but also energy and possibility.

Through practicing mindfulness meditation we can actively cultivate qualities that build our emotional resilience, in the same way that we exercise to improve our physical fitness. We can learn to handle difficult emotions more positively and to respond to experiences rather than being hijacked by them. We also become more attuned to positive experiences in our life. This book will show you how, as well as helping you to explore what the different feeling states mean to you.

There will be times when you forget to do your mindfulness practice, or perhaps you won't follow the week-by-week format rigidly. Both these are okay. You are here to explore for yourself how mindfulness might become a part of your life, and so the best attitude you can take is one of healthy skepticism. If you view the process as an experiment, you will have no expectation of a particular outcome but will remain open to whatever arises. Most importantly, cultivate an attitude of kindness and flexibility toward yourself. You can only do your best within the constraints of your daily life, so be gentle on yourself when things go awry.

TAKING CARE OF YOURSELF

If at any time a practice feels difficult or brings up strong feelings, please just stop. It's important that we always take care of ourselves, and sometimes it is helpful to learn mindfulness meditation with guidance from an experienced teacher. It is also better to begin practicing the ideas in this book when you are feeling well. As the mindfulness expert Jon Kabat-Zinn, who developed the secularized form of mindfulness says, weave your parachute so that it's ready when you might need it.

WHAT IS MINDFULNESS?

Children are inherently mindful, but as we get older it's a quality that many of us lose. We spend much of our time drifting through our days on automatic pilot, thinking about the past or daydreaming about the future.

When we think about the past there may be an element of regret—wishing we had done something differently or feeling that something positive is over. When we think about the future there may be anxiety, or a sense of dissatisfaction with where we are now. Such unease is the opposite of feeling calm.

We forget that the past has happened and cannot be changed, and that **the future will be determined by what we do now—in this moment.**

We can do something consciously in the present moment only if we are aware of what is actually happening in that moment. To bring that moment into our awareness we must deliberately pay attention to our experience as it is unfolding and—crucially—do so without judging it. This is mindfulness.

By regularly paying attention to our inner and outer experiences we begin to notice our habitual patterns of thinking and behavior. We notice the stories we tell ourselves about our experience, and how those stories make us feel physically and emotionally. We notice that **our interpretation of events—the story we spin ourselves—is influenced by the mood we are in.**

We begin to pay attention to what is going on in the body, and we can unpack "the experience" into separate strands of thoughts, emotions, and felt sensations. The experience is still present, but our awareness of each element introduces some space, and the curiosity we bring to the "unpacking" creates a sense of perspective; we relate to our experience differently, and that changes how we feel about it.

LET CURIOSITY BE YOUR GUIDE

I'd encourage you to view this process as an experiment. What you observe and note in these pages is your record of the experiment. The most successful experiments are carried out without any expectation of a particular outcome, but simply involve creating a set of circumstances and being curious about what happens. Try it for yourself.

We can cultivate the quality of mindfulness through regular meditation. That might take the form of *Watching the Breath* (see page 26) for a short period or it might be done more informally, such as by drinking a cup of tea or washing the car with mindful awareness.

By regularly practicing mindfulness we learn that we have a choice about how we respond to our experience, and that when we exercise that choice mindfully our experience changes.

It is important to acknowledge that **when we pay attention to our experience we may not like what we find, and it may feel the complete opposite of being relaxed. This is okay.** We are not expecting to feel a particular way, but rather learning to respond to all states of mind—not just the positive ones. Paradoxically, by letting go of the attempt to control our experience and keep the bad stuff at bay, and instead allowing it all in, we learn that we can be with the difficult things that come up in life. That makes us feel more relaxed, calm, and happy.

Through practicing mindfulness regularly we cultivate particular attitudes (see page 20), and as we become aware of the present moment we begin to notice all kinds of things (see page 48).

WRITING AS PRACTICE: EXPLORING INTENTION 1

Practicing mindfulness in a sustained way requires a substantial amount of motivation, and it's worth exploring what drives that motivation.

It could be that you would like to experience some of the therapeutic benefits of mindfulness, or perhaps you are just want to **live a life that is more present.** You may want to be less reactive or more compassionate to yourself. Many triggers bring us to mindfulness, and while specific goals are unhelpful—as they run the risk of introducing an element of striving and the idea that things are not good enough as they are right now—it is helpful from time to time to connect with the overarching intention that underpins our practice.

One way to do this is through writing practice. It can be helpful to begin with a period of sitting practice, perhaps just *Watching the Breath* (see page 26). Then bring to mind when you first heard about mindfulness, or perhaps remember a time when your interest was piqued. Silently ask yourself **"Why do I want to practice mindfulness?"** Let the question drop into your subconscious without any expectation of a particular answer. Every so often, repeat the question. Then bring

your attention back to the breath to close the sitting practice, pick up your pen and notebook, and begin writing practice.

Set a timer (use your phone, or your kitchen timer) for 3 minutes. There are just three rules:

1 **Don't stop.** Any time you hesitate or don't know what to write, just repeat the words "I want to practice mindfulness because ...".

2 **Don't edit your words or cross anything out.** There is no need to worry about handwriting, spelling, or grammar—anything goes! This is for your eyes only.

3 **Don't read what you are writing** until the timer has sounded.

When you have finished, read what you have written. Don't judge it, but simply read it as a practice. You may like to highlight particular words or phrases that stand out for you, or write a sentence or two in reflection.

I want to practice mindfulness meditation because ...

_____

_____

_____

_____

THE IMPORTANCE OF REFLECTING

Reflecting on experience can be very helpful, and jotting down some notes and observations is a good way to do it. Through reflection, we can take the opportunity to set an intention for our practice, a guiding star to which we can refer from time to time to make sure we are heading in the right direction.

It can be helpful to revisit our intentions periodically and make any adjustments as necessary, and there is an opportunity to do this on pages 12, 74, 182, and 184. There is more about exploring intentions on page 151.

We can also set specific goals—make a note of certain practices we'd like to explore and perhaps when and for how long we'd like to practice them. However, it's important that we view these flexibly and don't beat ourselves up when we don't manage to do what we had hoped. **It is always better to set realistic short-term goals than to make grand plans that do not come to fruition.**

Day to day, reflecting helps us to take a step back and notice what is coming up. It can be helpful always to check in with the three key areas, head, heart, and body: what do you notice? Even if there is nothing present, tune into all three every time; it is the act of tuning in that is important. Reflecting on what we notice helps us to identify patterns—helpful or unhelpful—that might arise in our thoughts and behavior. Through doing this over time we may begin to notice change, which can help to motivate us to continue our practice.

Some people like reflecting and write a lot, but journaling can be really simple and take the form of short notes:

MONDAY
"20 min sitting—mind all over the place. WORK!"

TUESDAY
"Mindful walking in the park. 20 mins."

WEDNESDAY
"Sat 10 minutes before breakfast. Felt settled. Noticed mind "planning" but kept on coming back to breath. Shoulders really tight. Noticed reacted less at work."

THURSDAY/FRIDAY
Skipped.

SATURDAY
"Didn't sit but had a mindful moment over my lunch in the park—sun on my face, first time this year."

SUNDAY
"15 minutes sitting. Checked work emails and noticed anxiety in evening—restless and sick feeling in stomach, thinking about tomorrow. Did a Breathing Space, closed down email, and had a long, hot soak instead."

We are all interested in different things. For some of us it's about how long we sit or how often, for others it's more about what we notice. **Be curious about what interests you and remember to bring that curiosity to your observations—letting go of any judging that arises (and not judging the judging either!).**

Alternatively, use the space in your notebook to record observations of a particular activity that you might be focusing on for the week. See it as an experiment, noting what you did, when, and for how long, and anything you noticed before, during, and after.

Some people prefer to doodle rather than write—or a mix of the two. It's your space, so use it however you wish.

TUNING INTO THE BODY

*"Mr. Duffy lived a short distance from his body." James Joyce's description in **Dubliners** could apply to many of us who spend an inordinate amount of time in the head.*

Although problem-solving can be a helpful strategy, it is less successful with emotional problems—and, in fact, can cause us to become stuck in a repetitive cycle of thinking or rumination. **We can't think our way out of emotional distress.**

When we are disconnected from the body we are disconnected from how we are feeling physically and emotionally. We may simply have got into the habit of intellectualizing our experience, or perhaps we have deliberately shut off our

experience because it feels unpleasant or painful. Not only does it use up a lot of energy to resist feeling something, but also we can't pick and choose what we feel, so we habitually begin to block out the pleasant feelings too. We are left feeling numb. Experiencing emotions and feelings are what make us feel alive (even if they are unpleasant).

We can redress the balance by deliberately reacquainting ourselves with the body; tuning into specific parts of the body and noticing what is—or isn't—there in terms of felt sensations. We are not looking for, or expecting to have, a particular experience, but simply being curious about our sensations. **It is the act of tuning in that is important, rather than what we discover.**

When we scan the body in this way we also become familiar with the power of the breath, learning to direct it into a very specific area, or expanding it and allowing it to hold our experience, whatever that may be.

THE BODY SCAN

1 Find somewhere comfortable to sit or lie down. Begin by settling your attention on the breath and noticing the sensations of breathing: the expansion and contraction of the lungs, and the rising and falling of the chest. Stay with this for several minutes. This is the place to which you will come back whenever your attention wanders or if things feel a bit tricky.

2 When you feel ready, take your attention down to the feet, specifically the big toes. Become aware of the big toe (first one and then the other, then both together), noticing any sensations that might be present (tingling, warmth, coolness …) or exploring the absence of sensation. Notice any thoughts or emotions that may arise, acknowledge them (for example "boredom is here"), and bring your attention back to focusing on the body.

3 Then move your attention to the other toes … and then the soles of the feet … the heels … the top of the feet. All the time be curious about this exploration, without expecting to feel a particular way.

4 When you are ready, direct your breath into and out of the feet: imagine that your feet are breathing and that the air is entering and leaving through the feet.

5 Do this for about a minute and then, letting go of the breath, take your attention to the ankles.

6 Continue in this way through the different areas of the legs: shin, calf, knees, thighs, hip … front, back, and sides. Then direct the breath up and down the length of the legs.

7 Then move to the pelvis ... the groin ... buttocks ... lower back ... middle back ... upper back ... shoulders ... belly ... chest.

8 Notice external sensations such as points of contact (or the absence of contact), an itch, or tingling, as well as any sensations within in the body.

9 Any time you realize your mind has gone for a walk, simply bring your attention back to the body.

10 Then move down the arms into the hands and fingers/thumbs, before moving up the arms (wrists, forearms, elbows, upper arms, shoulders).

11 Move to the neck (and internal throat) and take the attention along the jaw to explore the mouth, nose, eyes, forehead, temples, ears, skull.

12 Every time you complete a section of the body, imagine you are directing the breath into and out of that particular area.

13 When you have completed the head, imagine the breath entering through the head and leaving through the soles of the feet, so the breath is sweeping into one end of the body and out at the other.

14 Finish by expanding your awareness to include the whole body.

BEING WITH DISCOMFORT

If you feel strong sensations or even discomfort or pain as you do this practice, you have a choice about how to react. Experiment with the different options:

Option 1
You can direct the breath into that specific area, *breathing into* the discomfort.

Option 2
You can take your attention back to the place where you experienced the sensations of breathing at the start of the practice (the belly or chest) and, using your breath as an anchor, *breathe with* the discomfort … holding it in your awareness as you breathe in and out.

Option 3
You can be *curious about the discomfort* … moving in a bit closer to it and exploring it farther … Where exactly are you experiencing it? What kind of shape is the discomfort? Is it hard, soft, solid, insubstantial? Is it pounding, tingling, stabbing, throbbing? What is important here is maintaining an attitude of friendly interest, rather than analysis. You are simply exploring the territory of discomfort—remembering that you can always return to the breath at any time.

Option 4
Of course you can always adjust your position or move, but do so with awareness— that is, *know what you are doing while you are doing it*, rather than acting automatically and unconsciously.

CULTIVATING THE ATTITUDES

Key attitudes underpin and support our mindfulness practice. All these are cultivated through our "formal" meditation practice, but we can also encourage them in our daily life.

Curiosity is an important component of our practice. When we are curious about something we are interested in it, and when we are interested in something we want to explore it and find out more. This approach mode is the opposite of avoidance, and is crucial if we want to learn to be with difficulties in a different way. We can be curious about our own experience, our environment, and other people. Practice being curious and see what you discover.

Striving for a particular result is counterproductive in the practice of mindfulness, because we are learning to be with our experience right now, not sometime in the future. Striving has a driven quality to it—a harshness that suggests something is lacking, or that our situation (or ourselves) could be better. When we strive for something we focus on a single end, and constantly check to see how far we are from where we want to be. **Non-striving** feels more  spacious, and leaves room for unforeseen opportunities to arise. Paradoxically, we are more likely to reach where we want to be if we can let go of striving. Where do you strive in everyday life? What pressure do you put on yourself to achieve "XYZ" and how would it feel to let those aspirations go? Begin with something very small.

"In the beginner's mind there are many possibilities but in the expert's there are few." The well-known words of the Buddhist monk Shunryu Suzuki are worth bearing in mind. When we think we are an expert, we have a position to protect and defend. When we think we know it all, we are blind to what may actually be arising. **Can you approach your experience with "beginner's mind"?** Can you

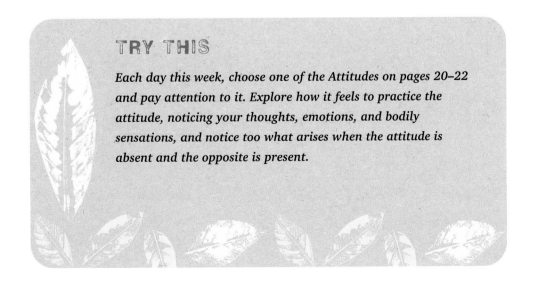

TRY THIS

Each day this week, choose one of the Attitudes on pages 20–22 and pay attention to it. Explore how it feels to practice the attitude, noticing your thoughts, emotions, and bodily sensations, and notice too what arises when the attitude is absent and the opposite is present.

see it as if for the very first time—drink this cup of tea as if you've never tasted it before? Try it now. What do you discover?

One of the first things we notice when we begin paying attention is how judgmental we are—of others and of ourselves.

Non-judging is at the heart of mindfulness. It is not easy to notice and acknowledge the judging thought, and then let it go. Gently labeling it "judging is here"—noticing the tone of your inner voice as you do so—can be helpful. There is nothing wrong with having an opinion about something, but notice whether there is a sense of righteousness about it? Pay attention to your judging mind (without judging it, of course).

Acceptance has to arise from within. Learning to accept when things are not as we would like them is never easy. However, we can learn this skill when we practice being with the itch on the end of our nose or the pins and needles in our feet when we sit, accepting that things are not as we would like them to be.

The benefit of giving yourself a whole year of mindfulness practice is that there is no rush. You have 52 weeks and 365 days ahead of you, so it is important to be patient with yourself when your practice falters and let change emerge in its own time. You may feel as though nothing is happening, but a lot bubbles below the surface as we practice. Notice when you are impatient in your everyday life: with the old lady shuffling ahead of you and blocking your way, or with someone new at work who hasn't quite grasped how things are done yet, so is taking twice as long as they should … Notice what that impatience feels like in your body, become aware of the accompanying thoughts, and breathe. Breathe and remind yourself that here is an opportunity to pay attention to the breath and to practice patience.

Kindness is at the heart of mindfulness. We must practice kindness when we falter in our practice, or when we are harsh with others or with ourselves. If being kind to yourself feels too much to ask, can you simply practice not being so mean to yourself? Can you treat yourself as you would your best friend?

REFLECT.....

_____

_____

_____

_____

_____

_____

SAVORING OUR EXPERIENCE

Attention informs our experience—helping us to notice what is actually going on—and it also transforms our experience, making it seem more vivid. Paying attention to how we nourish ourselves physically is a practice that is rich in feedback.

PREPARING YOUR FOOD

Pay attention to the process of preparation. **Explore the process with all your senses.** For example, when you are chopping vegetables, pay attention to the sensation of the knife in your hand, the rhythm of the chopping, the smell of the vegetables. What do you notice? How about the heat rising from the cooktop? The sound of the stock bubbling? The scent of the herbs?

EATING MINDFULLY

Experiment with eating and knowing that you are eating by exploring eating in silence and without reading, checking your phone, or looking around you. Engage all the senses. **What do you notice?** How do you feel during and after eating? How does this experience compare to your usual way of eating? What do you notice later on: how do particular foods affect your mood and physical well-being?

If our food is lacking in color, texture, taste, or smell, we will notice more acutely when we pay attention to it. This may encourage us to make healthier choices about what we are eating. Similarly, as we notice connections between certain foods and how we feel after eating them, we can begin to make informed choices about what we eat.

We don't need a whole meal to make eating or drinking part of our mindfulness practice. In fact it may be easier to begin with that mid-morning cup of tea or coffee and use that as an opportunity to come into the present moment. Whether you are at home or work, stop whatever else you might be doing and **simply be in the moment**—feeling the sensation of the cup in your hand—the temperature, the smell, and then taste. Notice if your mind gets pulled away into the past or future and when that happens (because it will), simply acknowledge it and bring it back to this moment. You may want to experiment with herbal teas that have intriguing scents and tastes to draw you in. Take 5 minutes of tea (or coffee) practice and then continue with your day.

See the *Mindful Eating* practice on page 56.

WATCHING THE BREATH

The breath is always accessible to us and has much to offer.
Its changing nature—fast, slow, shallow, deep—teaches us
to become familiar with changing states, and noticing what
comes before and after can give us helpful feedback.

When we regularly practice tuning into the felt sensations of breathing, the breath becomes an anchor for our distracted thoughts and emotions; **it becomes a place of safety,** a place to which we know we can return over and over again, and which will always be there. Some people find going to the breath too challenging; if this is the case for you, choose a different focus, such as your feet on the floor (see page 30).

We can watch the breath informally—during the daily commute, or while we are waiting for the dentist, sitting in a meeting, or standing in line—and we can also set aside a longer period of time for a more "formal" sitting practice. It is helpful to practice both ways, and the essential instructions remain the same:

1 **Identify the place where you feel the breath most strongly** in this moment (commonly the belly, the chest, or around the nostrils and upper lip), and set the intention that this place will be your focus of attention.

2 Begin noticing the sensations of breathing (this is different from thinking about breathing). **You are interested in what breathing feels like in this moment.** (It can be helpful to place a hand on your belly or chest to connect with these physical sensations—the rising and falling, the expansion and contraction.)

3 Sooner rather than later, your mind will wander. That is what minds do—it's part of their essential nature, and it is fruitless to try and stop it. However, **the moment you realize your attention is somewhere other than on your breath, acknowledge it.** (You can even say "thinking.")

4 Gently bring your attention back to the focus you identified at the start of the practice, and begin watching the breath once more. Stay with the length of each in-breath, notice the instant when an in-breath becomes an out-breath, follow the out-breath, and so on.

5 Your mind will go for a walk repeatedly, and the instruction is to bring it back each time without criticism or judgment. That is the essence of the practice. **By acknowledging that you are "thinking" and letting it go by bringing your attention back to the breath, you practice "unhooking" yourself from your thoughts.**

6 Continue in this way for as short or as long as you wish.

POSTURE: TAKING YOUR SEAT

When we watch our breath we make an intention to be with our experience in a different way from usual. We can support this intention by adjusting our posture.

If you are practicing informally, a balanced position is ideal: sitting or standing with both feet planted on the ground, allowing the crown of the head to rise toward the sky, so the torso is lengthened and uplifted.

If you are practicing more formally, do the same thing, but sitting on a chair or on the floor. If you are sitting cross-legged, the important thing is that your hips are higher than your knees (which may mean you need to sit on a pillow or block). If necessary, support your knees with pillows.

THE BENEFIT OF A BUSY MIND

The neural pathways for thought and paying attention to a physical sensation are the same, so we can't do both at once. Therefore, when we are really present with the physical sensations of breathing it is not possible for us to be "thinking" (although it's normal to become distracted again quickly). Paying attention to the breath is therefore a way to shift gears from "doing" mode (in the head) to "being" mode (in the body)—present moment awareness. Every time we make that shift we break the cycle of repetitive thinking and strengthen new patterns of thinking and behavior. That is why it is the repeated action of disengaging from thought and returning to the breath that is important. The busier your mind is, the more opportunity there will be to practice this important skill.

REFLECT....

_____

_____

_____

_____

_____

_____

BREATHING THROUGH THE FEET ON THE FLOOR

The more frequently we do something, the more likely it is to become embedded in the routine-oriented areas of the brain, and to become an unconscious action. This often happens with unhelpful behavior, but we can deliberately develop positive behavior that becomes so ingrained that we find ourselves doing it without consciously deciding to.

Breathing through the feet on the floor is something you can do at any time to ground yourself. It is particularly helpful when things are feeling tricky—perhaps if you are waiting to see the doctor, or before an interview or presentation—but if you can get into the habit of doing it when things are good as well, it will be easier to draw on in times of difficulty.

TRY THIS

Making sure both feet are planted firmly on the ground, drop your attention to the soles of the feet. In your mind's eye, imagine that you are breathing in and out through the soles of the feet. Keep your attention firmly on them, and if your mind wanders, simply bring it back. Continue for a few breaths, or for as long as you wish.

This week, do this practice as often as you can. You can schedule it three times a day, perhaps tagging it to activities you are already doing regularly, such as traveling to work, or sitting down to eat, or sitting down at your desk. Chances are that you won't remember, but the act of scheduling will mean that at some point you will think "feet on floor!" That is the moment to do the practice, wherever you are.

Reflect on when you have done this practice and what you noticed. What did you discover about scheduling the practice?

EXPLORING THE BEAM OF AWARENESS

Mindfulness is all about actively paying attention, but that attention can take different forms.

Sometimes it might be focused on a very small part of our experience, perhaps an itchy nose. At other times we may widen our attention to include the body and our environment: as well as being aware of our breath, the feet on the floor, and the body as a whole, we notice the sounds and smells around us, the air on our cheek, and what comes into our vision. Many of us have lost the habit of focusing, as we are bombarded by alerts and notifications on our phones and computers. Distraction is now our default state of being. When we practice formal meditation, we intentionally hone our attention and let go of distractions, but we can also do that in everyday life. This week, experiment with your attention: you might like to picture it as a beam of light that you can direct wherever you like. Sometimes the beam is tightly focused, and at other times it is wide. Play with switching between the two.

How wide can you go and still be aware of the sensations of breathing?
How focused can you be?
What do you notice in either mode?

This is something you can do any time and any place. Bring a sense of playfulness, rather than striving, to this practice.

REFLECT....

OPERATING ON "DEFAULT"

Autopilot can become our default operating system. It is an appealing mode to be in, as it demands little input from us, uses less mental energy, and allows us to zone out from the things we find difficult—the crowded commute, the boring job, or the homeless person sleeping in the doorway.

Sometimes autopilot is essential, as it helps us to complete regular tasks such as driving a car, getting the kids out of the door to school, or getting to work on time when we've slept through the alarm. However, operating on autopilot for the majority of our time exacts a heavy price.

Feeling happy and content arises from feeling good about life—a life made up of all the little things we experience. **When we zone out from the experiences we don't like, we are also tuning out any positive experiences:** the smell of rain on fallen leaves, the smile of a passerby, the feeling of the sun on your face, the beauty of a bunch of rainbow tulips, and so on. Since the mind has a bias toward negativity anyway (an evolutionary survival mechanism), tuning out positive experiences through being on autopilot creates a bleak picture of life. When we habitually zone out from all our experience, we become unaware of what we are thinking, what we are feeling emotionally, and what is happening in the body. We feel dead inside.

Since we operate automatically **when we are on autopilot, our emotions are more likely to be hijacked when our buttons are pressed**, and we will be in react, rather than response, mode. When we have a knee-jerk reaction we often regret it and wish we had behaved differently, and then we may get stuck in the trap of overthinking that is rumination. So the cycle of suffering continues. The opposite of zoning out is tuning in. We can tune in by paying attention to our experience, deliberately and without judging it. That is mindfulness.

Sometimes people say they prefer to tune out from their experience, because it's "easier" and "less unpleasant." "Why pay attention to the bad stuff?" they ask. **The choice is yours.** The present moment is the only moment we can influence what happens next—the future—unlike life on autopilot where we are passively carried wherever our reactions take us. If you are going through the days, weeks, and months of your life without being aware of them, are you really living or simply existing? Which would you prefer?

EXPLORING FELT SENSATIONS

Tuning into the body and exploring our experience is an integral part of mindfulness. However, many of us have become disconnected from the body, and we are unsure what we are experiencing—if anything at all. This week the invitation is to explore felt sensations in the body, without any agenda, simply with a spirit of curiosity.

What does "happy" feel like in the body? How about "tired" or "irritated"? Sometimes we struggle to find words to describe our experience, and different words may mean different things to each of us—see the word cloud opposite for some suggestions. Feel free to add your own. **Notice if there is a sense of judgment associated with your experience**. Is it good, bad, or neutral? We do this all the time, so it is useful to bring the process into our awareness.

The primary focus here is felt sensations in the body, but these are closely linked to thoughts and emotions so pay attention to those, too. Sometimes you may notice the sensations first; at other times the emotion or the thoughts may be what prompts you to pay attention to what you are experiencing in the body. Be curious about what you discover but avoid analyzing it.

What do you notice in terms of thoughts—do the sensations change in response to certain thoughts? **Can you name the emotions**?

By doing this you will become used to unpacking your experiences and aware of how they are made up of different sensations, thoughts, and emotions. This allows you to step back from what is going on and observe it, rather than getting caught up in it. You don't need to do anything with what you discover; simply be willing to explore.

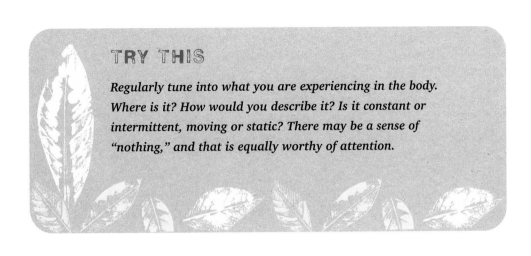

TRY THIS

Regularly tune into what you are experiencing in the body. Where is it? How would you describe it? Is it constant or intermittent, moving or static? There may be a sense of "nothing," and that is equally worthy of attention.

soft dead cold prickling stabbing tingling SOLID wispy loose warm itchy HEAVY STIFF NEEDLING scratchy **contracted** butterflies bubbly constricted throbbing HOT FUZZY **tight** insubstantial LIGHT numb

REFLECT....

_____

_____

_____

_____

_____

_____

SEVEN ... ELEVEN

Although this short practice is one that is taught to children, we can all benefit from it. Unlike the usual mindfulness of breathing instructions, this practice asks you to breathe in a particular way: in for the count of seven and out for the count of eleven. Try it now and see what you notice.

It may take some getting used to, particularly if your breathing is usually quite shallow. Don't struggle with it, but build it up over a period of time.

Practice "Seven ... Eleven" as often as you can this week. Sitting on the bus or in the car at a red light, waiting for your computer to boot up, or for your child to find that missing bit of school kit. Try to lengthen the out-breath. What do you notice?

1 2 3 4 5 6 7

1 2 3 4 5 6 7 8 9 10 11

MINDFUL MOVEMENT

Movement practice is a great opportunity to inhabit the body and explore what we are capable of (or not) in this very moment. Usually we move with a particular purpose in mind—to get from A to B, to become more flexible or burn calories, or perhaps to swim or run a particular distance. Mindful movement practice provides the chance to let go of striving and instead settle into where we are in the moment. When we practice "beginner's mind" we become open to the possibilities of this moment, regardless of how we "performed" previously.

The instructions opposite are for a walking practice, but the same principles can be applied to any other activity, such as running, swimming, or more traditional meditative practices such as yoga, tai chi, and qi qong.

When doing an activity as a mindfulness practice, experiment with the breath. Notice your relationship to it: are you holding it? Does it feel quick and panicky? Explore the "edge" (that place that feels as if you have reached your limit) with your breath. Pay particular attention to the out-breath and noticing how the body softens as you breathe out. **Remember always to take care of yourself, never push through pain, and respect the limits of your body.**

You can do a *Mindful Movement* practice at home—inside or out—and if it feels okay you can experiment with doing it barefoot. All you need is a short distance to walk up and down or in a circle.

1 Begin by making an intention to walk mindfully, that is, **intentionally become aware of your experience as it arises, without judging.**

2 If you can, take a moment to stand still and connect with the sensations of your feet in contact with the ground. Then form the intention to begin peeling your left heel off the ground, noticing how you feel as the foot lifts, shifts, and then is placed on the ground as you take a step.

3 Then, taking your attention to the opposite foot, begin peeling the heel off the ground, **lifting, shifting, placing ...**

4 Continue in this way, at first **keeping your attention focused on the feet on the floor** (bringing your attention back whenever it wanders in exactly the same way as you did when *Watching the Breath* on page 26).

5 **Experiment with walking at different speeds.** If you are walking very slowly you might prefer to do this in the privacy of your home to avoid raising comment with friends or neighbors!

6 From time to time, **widen your beam of awareness to include the whole body,** becoming aware of sensations within the body and perhaps the environment around you: sights, sounds, and smells.

7 You may also like to stop and stand still occasionally and notice what that feels like in the body.

8 **Be curious** about the experience of walking.

9 **Let go** of any agenda, goal, or seeking a particular outcome. Simply be with the experience as it is.

You can transform any walking you might do in your daily life into an opportunity to practice. The only reason we walk slower than usual in the formal walking practice is to remind ourselves that we are walking in a different way. When doing walking practice in our everyday life, the challenge is to walk without calling attention to ourselves and yet remember that we are walking as practice. Try it, and see what happens. Experiment with doing it slowly in the privacy of your home and then faster, out in the wider world. What happens to your attention? What do you notice?

CHOOSING A PRACTICE

When we feel agitated and anxious, sitting still can be too big a challenge. At such times *Mindful Movement* practice can be particularly helpful, either as a standalone practice or as a precursor to sitting practice.

REFLECT.....

_____

_____

_____

_____

_____

_____

SOUNDS

Sounds share many of their characteristics with thoughts: we can't control them, but instead they come and go, and some are stronger than others; we judge them, and can have a strong physical and emotional reaction in response to them.

We can fabricate a complex thought story around a noise, particularly if we are feeling particularly stressed or down. A noisy neighbor or a workman drilling outside the window can quickly seem like a personal affront.

Practicing being with sounds, therefore, provides excellent training for **being with our thoughts.**

This week, pay particular attention to sounds. Notice how the body picks up sound like a radar and, just like the rings on a radar, reverberates to sound. Pay particular attention when you notice this, following the physical manifestation of the sound in the body.

Notice how you judge a sound and the story you create around it, paying attention to the mood you are in and how this might affect your interpretation and thus your thoughts.

Acknowledge the story and then let it go by bringing your attention back to receiving the sound as a collection of notes at a particular pitch. Notice how a sound can trigger a thought, whether a memory of a past event

or person or a fear of something that is yet to happen. It seems instantaneous, and often we are unaware of what has triggered the change in mood. We can use music deliberately to lift our mood, and likewise we may wallow in sad songs that drag us down and down. When you notice this, nip it in the bud and change the tune.

Pay attention to the small sounds that are easily missed: the bird trying to out-sing a rival outside the window, the infectious giggling of a baby, or the sudden string of perfect notes as your child successfully masters a tune.

WHAT DO WE DO WITH NOISE THAT IS DRIVING US MAD?

This is when practicing on sound in general bears fruit. The instruction remains the same: notice the story you are telling yourself; acknowledge the emotions that are arising; notice how the noise manifests itself in the body; use the breath as an anchor when the story pulls you away. Keep coming back to the breath and the bodily sensations. The noise is not personal but simply a collection of notes that rise and fall. It is a collection of vibrations passing through the ear. Can you experience the noise as a harsh melody? Can you **be curious** about how the body responds to the cacophony of noise? **We don't have to like the noise; we simply want to explore a different way of relating to it,** letting go of the resistance to it and instead embracing it and moving toward it.

LISTENING MINDFULLY

When we communicate with others, a large part of our time is spent in our heads, rehearsing what we want to say, rather than paying attention to what is actually being said. For that reason, we often miss important information.

When we live in the head we are not present in the body, so we are ignoring an important opportunity to receive feedback on what we are hearing. This week, practice being present when you are listening.

- Stay present. When you notice your mind wandering bring it back, exactly as we do when we sit in meditation practice.
- Let the speaker finish without interrupting.
- Listening mindfully is much more than just listening with the ears. Notice the speaker's body language and facial cues as well as their tone of voice.
- If you notice yourself mentally "rehearsing" what you want to say, acknowledge it and let it go.
- Notice if there is a wanting to fix and make things better. Unless advice is specifically being sought, can you simply listen and be a witness to the other person's experience?
- Notice if there is a "me too" tendency. Although sometimes it can be helpful to know that others feel as we do, it is all too easy when listening to jump in and direct attention back to us, topping a story with one of our own that is bigger, better, or more dreadful.

LISTENING VS HEARING

Listening is intentional and active, as opposed to hearing, which is
the passive receiving of sound vibrations passing through the ear.
We can choose to listen—or not.

As you become more familiar with mindful listening, **practice widening your
awareness to include what you are experiencing in the body.**
Notice the felt sensations in response to what you are hearing. There may be a sense
of liking—softening, opening. Or perhaps there is a felt sense of resistance—
contraction in the belly, clenching in the jaw or hands. Whatever you notice is useful
feedback. If you become aware of a specific emotion, it may be helpful to view it as
a passing state: "anger is here" rather than "I am angry."

When we listen mindfully we maintain a wider perspective and are better able
to pick up cues that might hint at the history underlying the words that are being
spoken. We can acknowledge their pain and respond with empathy.

This isn't an easy practice, so be gentle with yourself when you forget and
interrupt. Do persevere, though, since it's a skill that benefits others as well as
yourself. How do you feel when someone really listens to you?

THE BENEFITS OF PRESENT MOMENT AWARENESS

When we are awake to our experience as it arises, we gain invaluable feedback on what is occurring. We become attuned to the body and its physical sensations, perhaps noticing sensations that arise in response to particular thoughts or emotions.

We are better able to untangle experience, so that, rather than being overwhelmed by a "bad feeling," we may discern the sensations and accompanying thoughts of the unpleasant feeling, and perhaps label the emotions that are present. In fairy tales, the unknown always has a power that is diminished once it is named. Labeling a strong emotion has been shown to activate the area of the brain that inhibits the automatic response associated with negativity and emotional reactivity, and can therefore dampen its effect.

When we notice and pay attention to the small pleasant experiences that are constantly available to us through the day, we "bank" them in the body memory. Reflecting later, **we have a more balanced view** and our life seems happier.

Regularly **tuning into the body gives us a familiarity with what is "normal" for us,** leaving us better attuned to any problems and able to take wise action. Through watching our changing experience minute by minute, hour by hour, day by day, we realize that "this too shall pass"—the good, the bad, and the neutral. Our states of mind are like passing weather fronts.

Awareness allows us to become familiar with our habitual patterns of thought and behavior, both those that are helpful and those that are not. We notice what nourishes us and what drains us. We can actively do more of the nourishing and explore ways to make the things that deplete us less draining. We become aware of the judging mind, which judges others and, more often, ourselves, constantly checking how we measure up against an imaginary scale of how it "should" be. Simply **letting go** of some of the meanness that we practice in our heads is a first step; actively practicing compassion for ourselves and others can be transformative.

A willingness to stand in someone else's shoes gives us an alternative viewpoint, allowing us to identify our individual biases with clearer sight, and make allowances for them. Rather than seeing situations and people in black and white, we become aware of all the shades of gray. A wider perspective helps us to see a problem for what it really is, without the additional stories we usually tell ourselves.

When we are present with others—giving them our full attention without being distracted by multitasking—we notice the benefit, and so do they.

When we do an activity with awareness—that is, knowing what we are doing while we are doing it—it becomes a richer and more vivid experience (even though we may not always like it). Good food eaten mindfully tastes amazing and bursting with flavors and textures, so we naturally start making healthier choices.

Bringing awareness to so-called routine activities can imbue them with new interest and energy. **When we pay attention we discover all kinds of things that would normally pass us by,** and when we are interested we are engaged and connected, rather than uninterested, bored, and disconnected.

Awareness and acknowledgment of our own vulnerability connect us with others, as "being human." We realize that suffering is not personal; it is not because we have "failed" or are "bad." We feel compassion for ourselves and for others. We acknowledge that we are all imperfect, and can only do our best.

A response that is borne out of the present moment is an active, engaged response, arising from a place of intention. When we truly acknowledge our experience in the present moment—whatever it is and regardless of whether we like it, want it, or think it's appropriate—we see clearly. It is only then that we can move forward from a position of knowledge rather than delusion.

WHAT ATTITUDES ARE YOU FEEDING?

Usually we experience a particular thought and/or emotion (it can be hard to determine which comes first) and then have thoughts about the feeling, perhaps finding evidence to support it or verbalizing it with catastrophizing language such as "what a nightmare."

In so doing, we stoke the fire so that the emotion flares up, perhaps out of control. Before we know it, anger or another emotion arises, we are at the mercy of an unconscious mind/body chain reaction, and the lack of control of the feeling (or the inability to understand where it has come from) can make us feel worse.

However, we do have the potential for control. Although we can't stop particular thoughts and emotions arising, through practice we can bring them into awareness. When we can **watch our thoughts** proliferate at the same time as becoming aware of their physical manifestation, we see how quickly they can become overwhelming. At first we may not be able to stop the unhelpful behavior, but simply noticing it is an important first step. We cannot do something differently until we bring it into awareness. Acknowledging that a particular emotion is present gives us the opportunity to choose how we respond and thus nip it in the bud.

Through practicing mindfulness we regularly **tune into our experience**, and so are more likely to pick up unhelpful behavior as it arises. Using our mindfulness practice we can notice the thought, emotion, or sensation, acknowledge and name it, and perhaps explore it gently using the breath and body to bring us into the present moment.

PRACTICING PATIENCE

Be patient and remind yourself that to begin with you may notice only after the event and wish you could have responded differently. This is perfectly normal; just continue practicing and noticing the emotions that you feed.

This week notice what behavior—**thoughts and emotions**—you feed. If you are feeling sad, perhaps you play soulful music that reflects your mood but also drags you down. If you are feeling fed up with work, you might indulge in water-cooler gossip to justify to yourself why you are right to be feeling that way. What could you do differently that might be more helpful?

REFLECT....

_____

_____

_____

_____

_____

_____

_____

_____

_____

_____

_____

_____

*Our awareness can increase rapidly,
so it is common in the early days to feel more
stressed by what we are noticing. As long as
we continue to practice, our perceived stress
will gradually reduce.*

APPRECIATING THE GOOD

We can redress our natural bias toward negativity by paying attention to pleasant experiences. There is no survival benefit in enjoying an experience, therefore they usually happen momentarily and are gone.

However, if we can bring that experience into awareness for as little as 60 seconds, we can bank it in our long-term memory. Make an intention to be aware this week of those fleeting moments of pleasure.

BANKING THE GOOD

Sometimes people are surprised at the way a seemingly insignificant experience creates a strong sense of pleasure, which they experience again when they reflect on it—an added bonus! Our natural negative bias means we usually forget a transitory pleasant experience—the warm sun on our face, the scent of a flower, the smile that lights up a child's face when they see us—but if we pay attention to the experience, noticing its different elements, we "bank" it in our long-term memory, and life starts to feel richer and more fulfilling.

Do this every day of the week if you can (or even better, continue beyond that). At the end of the period you've set yourself, think about what you notice. Reflect on any discoveries and insights.

What was the **experience**? What **thoughts** occurred to you?

What **felt sensations** did you notice in the body?

What **emotions** were you aware of?

What are you experiencing now as you write them down here?

Be as specific as you can.

MINDFUL EATING

How do you normally eat your food? When we pay attention to our eating habits we may notice that we usually eat while doing something else: perhaps watching television, checking our email or Facebook account, talking to someone else, or perhaps a combination of any of those. What do you notice about the experience of eating when you do this? How does the food taste?

Too often we eat mindlessly. We pay little attention to the experience of eating, and become disengaged from it. Because we are eating quickly, we are less likely to pick up the physical cues that we are full, and so eat too much. Since we are not present with the experience, we are depriving ourselves of the tastes, sounds, smells, and textures associated with it that add up to savoring the richness of the experience.

When we reach for the cookie jar or help ourselves from the fridge while on autopilot, we are not making an informed choice. When we are on autopilot, unhealthy patterns such as overeating in response to emotional crises are more likely to assert themselves.

You can begin to lay down healthier behavior patterns by choosing to make eating a practice:

1 Begin with preparing the food. Turn off the radio or television and give your full attention to what you are doing. Chop the onions and feel the smart in the eyes; experience the crunch of the celery, the fresh smell of the lettuce as you break it open. It doesn't matter what the food is, the instruction is simply to be present.

2 Notice the "ahhh yummy" or "icky, yuk" response of the body, becoming aware of any **thoughts, emotions, and felt sensations** that arise.

3 When you come to eat, if possible try to be silent. Give your full attention to the experience. Savor the smell, noticing the saliva in the mouth as the anticipation rises in the body. Make the intention to take a mouthful and be with that experience, chew it, and eventually swallow it. Continue in this way, **engaging all the senses: sight, sound, touch, taste, and smell.**

4 When you have finished, **reflect** on what you noticed.

PAUSING FOR CHOICE

When you find yourself reaching for that extra cookie or piece of chocolate, pause. Simply acknowledge what is happening without judging. Become aware of how you are feeling emotionally, any thoughts that might be present, and any physical sensations in your body. It is important that you don't judge yourself, but simply bring your attention to the breath, breathing in and out a few times before expanding your attention to include the whole body once more. Then, acknowledging all you have noticed, make a decision about what you want to do next. It is your choice and you are the only person who has the power to do something different in that moment. Whatever decision you make, be with it. So if you do choose the treat, be fully present with the experience of eating it, savor it, and let go of any judgment.

EXPERIENCING THE UNPLEASANT

This week, pay attention to those experiences you don't like. Notice when there is a sense of resistance, of "not wanting," "not liking," noticing any accompanying thoughts, emotions, and bodily sensations.

When you can, write down what the experience was together with what you noticed, and what you are experiencing as you reflect on it.

Would you normally have noticed any of this?

WHAT IS IT?

WHAT THOUGHTS ARE ARISING?

CAN YOU NAME ANY EMOTIONS?

WHAT ARE YOU NOTICING IN THE BODY?
BE AS SPECIFIC AS YOU CAN.

When something unpleasant happens, can you identify where you usually feel it in the body? How did this exercise compare with becoming aware of pleasant experiences?

REFLECT....

_____

_____

_____

_____

_____

_____

MOVING OUT OF YOUR COMFORT ZONE

As we get older, many of us become increasingly bound by our habits and routines. We've worked out a particular way to do something or get somewhere, and it's easier to repeat the action rather than do something different. This makes sense, since routine activities use up less energy in the brain and knowing what our experience is means fewer unpleasant surprises. However, much of our unhappiness with life arises when things don't go according to plan.

We can improve our resilience by deliberately moving out of our comfort zone and doing something different. By practicing with small inconsequential things, we can build up our tolerance gradually.

Make a list below of things you always do the same way. Perhaps you always sit in the same chair, travel the same route to work, or read the same newspaper.

Then choose one thing to do differently each day. You may want to start with something that feels easy and build up to something more challenging.

Be curious—this is an experiment, so approach it without any expectation of a particular outcome. "Beginner's mind" and "curiosity" are very helpful attitudes to employ (see pages 20 and 21).

Pay attention to what you notice arising before, during, and after your experience of doing the activity differently. What did you notice in the way of thoughts, emotions, and felt sensations in the body? If challenging sensations arise, name them ("fear is here," for example), notice any physical manifestation of the emotion and thoughts, and **use the breath as an anchor** to the present moment.

If doing something different feels particularly challenging on the first attempt, perhaps revisit it another time and see how that experience unfolds. **Notice whether the previous experience colors and influences your attitude the second time round and remind yourself to practice beginner's mind.**

WAKING UP WITH THE UNFAMILIAR

Varying our routines doesn't just build flexibility in our attitudes, it also wakes us up. When we go on vacation, everything seems interesting because it is different. We pay attention to our environment because it is unfamiliar and are consequently more present. We may try unexpected things, learn new skills, or reconnect with old ones. The experience feels richer because of all these factors. We grow only when we learn something new, and we learn something new only when we do things differently from normal.

HOW BEST TO SUPPORT YOUR PRACTICE

Maintaining a mindfulness meditation practice is challenging; it requires an ongoing commitment to be willing to turn toward the difficulties that most people do their best to avoid. You can support yourself in different ways.

FORMAL PRACTICE The formal meditations (see pages 16, 26, 40, 70, 102, 128, and 156) teach key skills, including tuning into the body, letting go of distractions and returning to a focus, and directing the breath in different ways. These skills are transferred into everyday life and will help in difficult situations. It isn't possible simply to tell yourself not to react to something; **the ability to pause and respond arises out of practicing formal meditation regularly,** and that is why it is important.

LOCATION Find a place to practice where you are unlikely to be disturbed. It can be helpful to exclude pets and to enlist the help of family and friends, explaining that your practice will benefit them as well as you. **Remember that you don't need silence to practice.** Learning to be with things not being as you would like them is a key component of mindfulness, so a barking dog, passing sirens, or bickering children in the next room are all grist to the mill.

POSTURE There is no need to sit cross-legged in the lotus position to meditate; a simple upright chair will do just as well. Make sure your feet are firmly grounded (you may want to place them on a pillow or pile of books) and that you are sitting upright and relaxed, yet alert. Your eyes can be open or closed: if you have them open, just soften your gaze, looking down and slightly ahead. If sitting is a challenge it's fine to lie down, but you may have to contend with sleepiness.

ROUTINE There is no perfect time of day to practice, but many of us benefit from incorporating our practice into our routine. It helps us remember to do it, and because it is regular we don't have to reorganize anything to make it happen. It becomes something that we just do—like brushing our teeth.

PRACTICING IN A GROUP Doing this alone without the support of a group or a teacher can be difficult. There is something special about practicing with others, and you will also benefit from the wisdom of the group or an experienced teacher. You can look for a local sitting group (or start your own at home), or for short courses or retreats, which may be for a day or longer.

PROGRESS It can be helpful to revisit your intentions from time to time, but avoid constantly judging your practice. **There is no good or bad meditation.** Sometimes you will sit with a busy mind or a restless body, at other times you will feel more settled, but neither state is better than the other; a busy mind does not make a meditation bad but rather is an opportunity to practice repeatedly letting go of the thoughts and returning to a focus such as the breath.

Your practice will wax and wane as your home and work life present different demands, but you can keep some element of practice going at all times with informal practices such as *The Breathing Space* (see page 88). Remind yourself that if you have gone for a period without practicing, you simply **start from where you are, by paying attention to this breath, this one that you are taking right now.**

TECHNOLOGY There are digital resources that will support your practice with downloads, CDs, apps, and timers. Some pop up from time to time as memory aids to remind you to come into the moment; others provide timed periods of practice, which may be guided or not.

Remember: doing a little often is better than practicing for an hour or so once a month!

REFLECT....

_____

_____

_____

_____

_____

_____

NOTICING THE NARRATIVE

As we become more used to observing our thoughts in our meditation practice, we start noticing how the same old stories seem to come up time and time again, both in our practice and in everyday life. These may be "poor me" or "I'm not good enough" stories, or perhaps something about our current job or situation—the list of possibilities is never-ending.

The story we tell ourselves will be influenced by our frame of mind. If we are feeling down it will be negative, whereas if our mood is good it will have a more positive spin. This fact alone tells us that we can't take our thoughts as facts.

This week, pay attention to the stories you tell yourself.

- Notice how your **mood influences your interpretation** of an experience.
- Become **aware of your posture,** paying particular attention to your jaw (is it relaxed or clenched?) and your hands. How are your shoulders? Notice your expression: are you frowning?
- **Tune into the body** and become aware of any sensations that are arising in response to the story (and then notice if new thoughts arise about those sensations). Of course, there may be none.
- When you become aware of a recurring thought, it can be helpful to bring some **lighthearted humor** to naming it: For example, thinking "Anxious Annie is here again!" will help you to distance yourself from your anxiety.
- Are you feeding a particular story, perhaps stoking it with righteous indignation? We can't control our thoughts, but **we can control how we**

respond to them. Those we feed will flourish and proliferate.

● If you notice a particularly self-critical story arising, let go of judging the judgment! Break the cycle by bringing your attention to the breath in that moment.

● **Noticing the feeling tone of your thoughts** can be a helpful indication of your state of mind.

Exploring the body and the physical manifestation of the thought and/or emotion can be a helpful way to disengage from the "doing" mind. We can also use the breath as a way of shifting our attention away from a particular focus. We do this all the time when we meditate, but we can do it when we are going about our daily life, as well.

What story is at the top of your hit parade this week?

1 _____

2 _____

3 _____

4 _____

5 _____

6 _____

7 _____

8 _____

9 _____

10 _____

REFLECT....

_____

_____

_____

_____

_____

_____

CREATING A SPACE

*By taking a **Breathing Space** we pause
and take a moment to acknowledge what is
happening in that moment.*

This is an opportunity to come into the present moment, to notice and acknowledge how things really are (rather than how we would like them to be), and with that feedback decide what it would be helpful to do next—if anything at all.

The Breathing Space (see page 88) is a versatile practice, but for now the main thing is to become familiar enough with it that you find yourself doing it several times a day.

As it can be tricky to remember to do *The Breathing Space*, you might want to schedule it a certain number of times a day. For example, it can help to "hook" it on to meal times. The more often you can do it, the more natural it will become for you to do it regularly throughout your day.

This week, practice *The Breathing Space*. Schedule it three times a day. Chances are you will still forget, **but at some point you will remember that you have forgotten—that is the moment to do The Breathing Space!**

Remember to be alert to a secret desire to "fix" or make yourself feel better. If it arises, notice and acknowledge it, but let it go. *The Breathing Space* is simply an opportunity to connect with what we are experiencing in *this* moment.

MINDFULNESS OF BREATH AND BODY

*When you have some experience of **Watching the Breath** (see page 26), you can extend the practice to include mindfulness of the body. This is one to do in a place where you are able to sit undisturbed for 10 minutes or longer.*

When we watch the breath we practice letting go of thoughts and using the breath as an anchor for our attention, albeit an 'elastic' tether that at times stretches quite far.

When we pay attention to what is arising in the body several things happen:

- The natural human response to discomfort or pain is to do anything we can to make it go away as quickly as possible. However, some physical sensations associated with accident or illness (physical or psychological) may not go away easily, or at all. **We can't get rid of the pain, but we can learn to change our relationship with it.** We notice the narrative we are creating around the pain and how we are "feeding" our suffering, and we can learn to let that go. In this way, our suffering is reduced. We learn how to live with things not being as we would like them to be in this meditation by practicing responding to minor discomforts, such as an itch on our nose, in a different way from usual. This gives rise to the "pause" between cause and effect that in everyday life is enough to allow us to respond wisely, rather than react automatically, to a difficult situation. We can't force ourselves to remember to do this pause; it arises naturally as a result of regularly practicing mindfulness of the breath and body.

- **We learn to use the breath to support us** in being with physical sensations we don't want.

- We practice tuning into the body and what is arising within it. This is the opposite of experiential avoidance, which is a characteristic of depression and indeed common with anyone who is experiencing chronic pain. **Regularly tuning into the body** gives us important feedback on our well-being.

- We learn to use the body as a way of grounding ourselves—getting out of the head and into this body, right now.

Begin by taking a seat and allowing yourself to settle by *Watching the Breath* (see page 26).

1 When you feel ready, expand your awareness outward from the breath to the entire body. Notice the parameters of your body sitting here (the feet, legs, torso, arms, head).

2 Gradually allow yourself to become aware of any physical sensations. These may be internal—a rumbling belly, or tingling or numbness in the extremities— or external—the sense of contact with floor, chair, or clothing, of warmth or cool, or of air touching skin. There is no need to hunt for sensations, but **simply be open to whatever arises.**

3 Notice whether you are judging a sensation as "pleasant," "unpleasant," or "neutral." How do you know? What is the felt experience of something unpleasant or pleasant? Become curious about how you tell the difference, perhaps noticing a tightening of muscle, a sense of hardness or resistance, or the opposite, a softening and opening with a sense of "ahh … I like that!" How do you respond when it is neutral?

4 Become curious about the characteristics of any sensation. Decide how to describe it: tingling, stabbing, sharp, numb … What shape is it? Is it solid or insubstantial, shifting or static? When we are interested in something we pay attention to it. Invite yourself to be interested in any physical sensation—good, bad, or neutral.

5 **Play with the breath.** Practice breathing into the sensation by imagining your breath as a narrow beam of light, shining on that area as you breathe in

and out. Alternatively, keep your attention focused on your breathing (in your belly or chest), being aware of the physical sensation as you breathe in and out.

6 You can also choose to adjust your position if necessary, but do it with awareness. That is, make a clear intention to move and then be aware of the experience of adjusting and settling into your new position.

7 Use any one of the above options or a combination at different times during your practice.

8 Continue for your designated time, and when you are ready to end, bring your attention back to the breath and where you started for a moment or two.

EXERCISING THE MUSCLE OF AWARENESS

Be patient and gentle with yourself; gritting your teeth stoically in the face of discomfort is not helpful. Notice what happens when you do that. It involves a stiffening of the muscles around the pain, and repeatedly doing it creates tension and stiffness in the body. This practice involves learning new habits that are counterintuitive to everything you've done before, so practice patience. At first you may be able to be with the "itch" only for a second or two before scratching it, and that's okay. Every time you do something different you exercise that muscle of awareness, but it is important not to be self-critical if and when you do "scratch the itch."

WRITING AS PRACTICE: EXPLORING INTENTION 2

Regularly checking in with what you are learning and noticing can be a very helpful way to motivate your practice. Begin with a period of sitting practice, taking the time to settle the attention on the breath. Then, when you feel ready, silently ask "How does my practice serve me?" Let the phrase drop into your subconscious like a pebble down a deep well. Notice any reverberations in the mind or body without having particular expectations; simply allow whatever comes up to do so. Repeat the question every so often. Continue for perhaps another 10 minutes or so.

Then set a timer for 35 minutes, pick up your notebook and pen and write down what you noticed. **Remember the three golden rules:**

1 **Don't stop.** Any time you hesitate or don't know what to write, just repeat the question.

2 **Don't edit your words or cross anything out.** There is no need to worry about handwriting, spelling, or grammar—anything goes! This is for your eyes only.

3 **Don't read what you are writing** until the timer has sounded.

When you have finished, read what you have written. Don't judge it, but simply read it as a practice. You may like to highlight particular words or phrases that stand out for you, or write a sentence or two in reflection.

REFLECT.....

_____

_____

_____

_____

_____

_____

_____

_____

_____

_____

_____

_____

"One must endure the caterpillars if one is to become acquainted with the butterflies."

Antoine de Saint-Exupéry, *The Little Prince,* 1943

THE POWER OF ATTENTION

When we are bored by something, we are not interested in it; we don't engage with it, and there is a sense of dissatisfaction that causes us to zone out. When we zone out of our experience, we are more likely to retreat into our thoughts, whether those are about the activity or something else. When our mood is low, we are more likely to switch on negative thinking, which then compounds the low mood, and so on.

What activities do you habitually zone out from or even dislike? These may be activities that are viewed as chores—loading or emptying the dishwasher, doing the dishes or the laundry, cleaning the toilet, taking out the trash, clearing the table, picking up after the children, washing the car … your list probably goes on.

Choose one activity that you don't particularly enjoy and start paying attention to it. Be curious about the experience:

- What emotions are present? Perhaps there is a feeling of resentment or dislike. Whatever is present, **acknowledge it** as what you are experiencing in this moment.
- What story are you telling yourself about the activity? Notice any connections between the story and any emotions and sensations but avoid analyzing.

Acknowledge whatever is arising (even if you think you "shouldn't be having" such thoughts).

- Pay attention to your breath and any sensory experience that arises from the experience: taste, touch, smell, sight, and sound. Use the senses to bring you back to the present moment whenever your thoughts and emotions pull you away.
- Mentally connect with all those other people in the world who are carrying out exactly the same task day after day. You are one of millions of human beings doing this very thing, perhaps at this very moment, and perhaps feeling the same way about it.
- Investigate whether there is another way to relate to the task. Perhaps you can think about who benefits from this activity. Try to see what you do as an act of love or affection for someone you care about, or perhaps simply as a contribution to the community of which you are part.

We don't have to enjoy what we are doing, but we can choose to relate differently to it.

CHANGING YOUR BRAIN!

Just as we can work out to increase the physical fitness of the body, so we can do a brain workout by practicing mindfulness meditation. Much of the research has been done with people practicing over a period of eight weeks and meditating for about 30–40 minutes a day, although benefits such as a reduction in perceived stress have been shown with shorter periods of practice, and it's possible that regularity of practice is the important thing. Certainly, when we engage in activities over and over again, the particular neurons involved change the way they communicate with one another as a result of experience. As the neuropsychologist Rick Hanson says, "neurons that fire together wire together."

The benefits reported by people practicing mindfulness meditation include:

- Decrease in rumination—the "hamster wheel" cycle of repetitive thinking.
- Reduction in anxiety.
- Reduction in perceived stress.
- Increase in empathy.
- Increase in self-compassion.
- Improvement in the ability to handle difficult emotions.
- Increase in happiness.
- Improved quality of life.

These reported psychological benefits are supported by physical changes in the relevant areas of the brain. In 2010, the neuroscientist Sara Lazar and her colleagues did a series of "before" and "after" brain scans of a group of non-meditators learning mindfulness meditation. The second set of scans, done after the subjects had spent eight weeks meditating for 30–40 minutes per day, showed that several areas of the brain had increased gray matter suggesting greater activity:

LEFT HIPPOCAMPUS This is the area of the brain that assists learning, memory, and emotional regulation. **Practitioners of mindfulness commonly report improved focus and attention and better decision-making.** People who suffer from depression or post-traumatic stress have less gray matter in this area.

An earlier study by Richard Davidson and colleagues done with healthy volunteers in 2003 showed that eight weeks of practicing mindfulness meditation caused a shift toward the left-sided activation of the brain—the area that is better able to handle difficult emotions—as well as a boost in the immune system that correlated with the degree of change to left-sided activation.

TEMPOROPARIETAL JUNCTION This area behind the ear is concerned with perspective, empathy, and compassion. Meditators commonly report feeling **greater empathy and compassion** toward themselves and others.

The ability to have a wider perspective on a situation encourages a more balanced viewpoint. Someone who feels threatened will see things from a narrow perspective, and their fear will influence their interpretation of events.

AMYGDALA One area of the brain that showed a reduction in gray matter was the amygdala, which is responsible for activating the fight or flight response (see page 93). The reduction in gray matter correlated directly with a reduction in the level of stress experienced. This physical change supports the fact that meditators report a reduction in perceived stress.

Another study by Lazar and her colleagues showed that mindfulness meditation may slow down the cortical thinning that usually occurs with age. Compared to a control group, scans showed that the brains of 50-year-old meditators had a similar thickness of cortical gray matter to those of 25-year-olds.

REFLECT.....

_____

_____

_____

_____

_____

_____

_____

_____

_____

_____

_____

_____

No one else can do this for you. Only you have the power to change this moment.

BEING PRESENT IN MIND AND BODY

A sign outside a café read: "No WiFi—Please talk to each other instead." Although it raised a smile it is unfortunate that it is now too often the norm to meet up with friends or family and spend the time with heads down checking the latest update on our phone, or perhaps taking pictures to upload instantly and show our virtual friends what a wonderful time we are having. When we are somewhere else mentally, we might as well not be present physically. When we are not present with someone, they may feel neglected and ignored.

This week, **practice being present** with friends, family, and colleagues.

● Turn off your phone and put it out of sight. Having it on the table next to you gives a message that something may take precedence over your time with this person.

● **Notice** where your mind goes. Every time you are aware of it drifting off, bring it back in the same way as you do when you meditate.

● Notice whether any particular emotions are arising—perhaps restlessness or the wish to be somewhere else. Whatever comes up, **acknowledge** it, tune into the body, and explore any sensations that accompany it.

● Practice *Listening Mindfully* (see page 46).

● **Reflect** on how being present with someone both physically and mentally affects the encounter and the relationship. What do you notice?

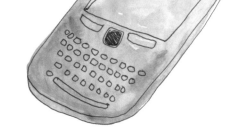

REFLECT....

_____

_____

_____

_____

_____

_____

SEEING WITH FRESH EYES

I was having lunch at a friend's home and enjoying the cheese I had spooned from a little dish on to my salad. "This is delicious," I said. "What is it?" She looked at me, a bit puzzled. "It's cottage cheese," she replied. I laughed because I hate cottage cheese! Or so I thought, anyway. However, experiencing it free of packaging— with "beginner's mind"—I discovered that I loved it. So it is with much of life.

Why bother? Why not avoid cottage cheese or its equivalent for the rest of my life? Apart from the risk that you will be missing out on something that you might actually enjoy, too often we become attached to a particular label or idea we have of ourselves. It becomes part of who we are—how others see us and how we view ourselves. **This can prevent us from growing,** from shedding out-of-date dislikes, habits, and behavior.

What is on your hit list of "things to avoid"? Write them down. Then choose something from that list and **try experiencing it as if for the first time.** Explore it with as many of your senses as possible. Pay attention to any resistance that arises in the form of thoughts, memories, emotions, and bodily sensations. Tease apart your experience. What do you notice? This is not about forcing yourself to like it—you still may not—but rather to see it with **fresh eyes.**

REFLECT.....

_____

_____

_____

_____

_____

_____

THE BREATHING SPACE

The Breathing Space *is the practice many people find most useful. It is a helpful bridge between the longer "formal" practices and the informal practices we can weave into everyday life. However, it should be more than just "time out," and rather be an opportunity to acknowledge what is going on in that moment.*

Unfortunately, many people skip that first stage, and jump straight into being with the breath. It is crucial to make an honest acknowledgment of our experience in this moment. It doesn't matter if we think that experience is wrong, inappropriate, or anything else; owning it is what is important.

Once we are familiar with *The Breathing Space*, we can do it when we are feeling stressed or if things are tricky. We can even take it a stage further (see pages 125 and 160).

There are three stages to this simple practice. It can be useful to repeat silently to yourself "step **1** … step **2**," and so on.

1 **Ask "What's up for me right now?"** Check in with your head (thoughts), heart (emotions), and body (felt sensations). Keep it short, and label what you discover. Sometimes there may be more than one emotion, for example.

2 Take your attention to the sensations of breathing. Perhaps repeat silently to yourself **"Breathing in … breathing out …"** as you follow each breath. This stage can be as long or as short as you like.

3 Expand your attention from the breath first to include the whole body. Become aware of points of contact with the floor, seat, or bed, or with other sensations, and then notice the environment—sounds, smells, the touch of air on skin … Continue with your day.

DITCH THE LABELS

Last week's challenge was to look at something you habitually avoid and experiment with seeing it with fresh eyes. This week the invitation is to take it a step farther: can you drop the filters that obscure your vision and instead see yourself as you actually are, right now?

How would you describe yourself? Do you use a particular label that is out of date? Perhaps you commonly think of yourself as someone's parent, or define yourself by your job; maybe you have a chronic condition that has taken over your life, or that makes you live life more circumspectly; maybe you describe yourself as "shy" or "no good at sport."

Labels can be useful, but by definition they are limiting. Each of us is the sum of many parts, and it's easy to hang on to familiar descriptions because the alternative—the unknown—seems scary. **Sift through any of the labels you use** (we all have them), and select just one to explore mindfully.

When you bring this description of yourself to mind, what do you notice? Become aware of any thoughts, emotions, and physical sensations. Explore your experience with an attitude of curiosity.

Can you experiment with **letting go** of whatever the label might be? When you imagine this, notice what comes up for you. This week, really pay attention to labels—those you use for yourself and perhaps also for others.

REFLECT....

_____

_____

_____

_____

_____

_____

STRESS AND HOW IT AFFECTS US

When we react negatively to an event we experience stress. Our heart rate increases, we may feel flushed, our palms may become clammy, and we may feel nauseous or need to go to the bathroom. This is evidence that the body's stress response—the sympathetic nervous system—is working: a threat has been identified, the alarm has sounded, and the body's defenses move into battle stations.

That's good news! If the body's internal alarm wasn't working properly, we would be at risk from potential stressors.

POSITIVE STRESS: Stress can be positive. **Positive stress (eustress) motivates us; it focuses our energy and feels exciting.** The body rises to a challenge and our performance improves. Positive stress is usually fleeting, and while it causes us to experience the same physical sensations as those generated by negative stress (distress), they are less damaging.

Feeling stressed from time to time is nothing bad, therefore, and it can be a sign that our body is helping us to perform at our best. It is only when we feel stressed constantly—negative stress—that problems may arise.

NEGATIVE STRESS: This feels unpleasant and is perceived as taking us beyond our coping skills. **It inhibits our performance, as we are operating from a position of anxiety and fear.** The stress reaction releases stress hormones, such as cortisol, that inhibit the neural branching of neurons in the brain and cause atrophy in the area of the brain responsible for developing new brain cells; effectively, our brain is not developing or functioning at its best. Cortisol also activates the amygdala, the brain's "alarm" button. All this combines to keep us stuck in fearful thinking. Negative stress can lead to mental and physical problems and can be short- or long-term (the latter is known as chronic stress).

THE STRESS REACTION: When the body identifies a potential threat, the amygdala (the most primitive part of the brain) sounds the alarm and the body releases stress hormones to aid in fight or flight, diverting all resources to this end. Long-term bodily functions such as digestion and reproduction are shut down, and energy is diverted from the higher centers of the brain (the "executive" functions), which require a lot of resources, to the most primitive areas, which focus purely on survival. Therefore, all decision-making now occurs from a place of fear and threat, and is devoid of higher "executive" function.

At the same time, the body continues to gather information from the higher reaches of the brain—accessing memory and stored information—as well as farther input from the senses to determine the level of threat. This is the crucial choice point, as **our thoughts can either end or maintain the alert.** If we are caught in a cycle of negative thinking, the threat level will be maintained and possibly even escalated. However, if we can change our perception (our thoughts), we have the ability to stand down the body's defense mechanism and activate the calming response, the body's built-in mechanism for returning to homeostasis (balance).

The more often the stress reaction is activated, the more sensitive the body becomes to triggers. We become hyper-vigilant for any possible threats. It takes the body about 90 minutes to recover from the effects of the stress reaction, so if it is constantly being activated, there is no time to recover, and the stress hormones cause continuous havoc in the body, disrupting all the usual functions.

Stressors may be external (people, situations, chemicals—such as drink or drugs—and viruses) or they may be internal, such as rumination (getting stuck in unhelpful thinking), fear and anxiety, unrealistic expectations, or perfectionism.

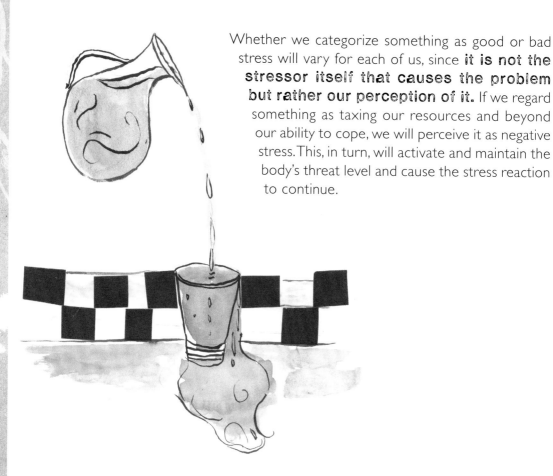

Whether we categorize something as good or bad stress will vary for each of us, since **it is not the stressor itself that causes the problem but rather our perception of it.** If we regard something as taxing our resources and beyond our ability to cope, we will perceive it as negative stress. This, in turn, will activate and maintain the body's threat level and cause the stress reaction to continue.

THE CALMING RESPONSE

When the calming response (the parasympathetic nervous system) is activated, the heartbeat and breathing slow, muscles relax, and the digestive juices begin flowing again. **The calming response is designed to promote growth, energy, and all the other processes that are needed for our long-term survival and well-being.** It is the opposite of the stress reaction.

We can learn ways of activating the calming response deliberately the instant we feel stressed, or even to nip stress in the bud if we are aware enough to pick up the early signs by tuning into our physical sensations. This could be by focusing on the breath, for example (see page 27) or breathing through the feet on the floor (see page 30).

We can also learn ways to **live more calmly day to day,** changing our perception of our experience and thereby inhibiting stress from arising in the first place.

When we are stressed, physical exercise will dispel the stress hormones released as part of the sympathetic nervous system's "fight or flight" reaction, as will crying.

IDENTIFYING YOUR STRESS TRIGGERS

Whether we perceive something as exceeding or taxing our resources determines whether it is a stressor. Stressors will be different for each one of us, and may even vary for us day by day. By identifying our common triggers, and how we behave and what we feel when we are stressed, we can develop our own early-warning system. This will help us to pick up early signs that we are running on empty, and take wise action.

What makes me stressed? (These may be individuals, situations, events; be as specific as possible.)

What do I feel physically when I'm stressed? (Ask yourself where you are feeling it, what kind of sensation it is, and how you would describe it. Be specific.)

_____

_____

_____

How do I behave when I'm stressed? (Notice whether particular emotions, such as anger or irritation, increase. Some of us sleep or eat more—or perhaps less—when we are stressed. We may drink to excess or take drugs (prescription or otherwise). We may curtail or stop hobbies and activities like sport or meeting friends. What do you notice about any changes in your behavior? Be specific.)

_____

_____

_____

What positive things could you do when you are stressed? (These could be small things, such taking a long, hot bath, going for a walk, or calling a friend. Think about what nourishes you when you are feeling stressed. Be specific.)

_____

_____

_____

_____

THE POWER OF TECHNOLOGY

Technology is supposed to make our lives easier, and in many ways it does. However, from time to time it is worth paying attention to our relationship with technology—texting, email, and social media—and noticing our attitude toward it. Dependence or over-use can creep insidiously into our lives.

This week, begin to pay attention to how you relate to things like email, Facebook, Twitter and all the other applications that are available to us through our computers, tablets, and cellphones.

Notice how often you check your email and social media. Does it feel as if you are doing it automatically? Is there a driven quality to the checking? Pay attention if you can to that moment of impulse. What thoughts do you notice? What emotions? How does it feel in the body? How do you feel afterward? Can you connect with any felt sensations or emotions that you experience?

Notice if there are particular applications that cause more upset than others. How does checking work emails out of office hours affect you? What do you notice when you read posts from family or friends?

Be awake to cause and effect.

Once you have a sense of whether technology is helping or hindering, you can decide whether you need to take wise action.

If it's the latter, you can use it as an opportunity for practice by bringing the moment of impulse into awareness. Can you allow yourself to experience the impulse without acting on it?

Use the breath to steady yourself and be curious about what the impulse is made up of. What drives it? What does it feel like?

Try to ride out the impulse three times before giving in to it (if you still want to).

Of course you can also use the device itself to aid you by turning off notifications or removing an app from your phone so that it can't be easily accessed, but if you do so you will miss an opportunity to strengthen your resolve and weaken your reactivity.

Remember, technology should serve rather than enslave.

REFLECT.....

_____

_____

_____

_____

_____

_____

_____

_____

_____

_____

_____

_____

"People are disturbed not by a thing but by their perception of a thing."

Epictetus (AD 55–135), Stoic philosopher

BEING WITH SOUNDS AND THOUGHTS

Sounds and thoughts share many characteristics. We have no control of either—a door slams, the neighbor's little boy jumps up and down in the apartment above, or a car alarm shrieks on and on … perhaps the strains of a song from your past drift in at the window. Some sounds are fleeting; others are not. They can make us angry, frustrated, or maybe nostalgic or happy.

As these emotions arise we may notice how the body responds: a clenching of the stomach, a tightness in the shoulders, a prickle behind the eyes, a rising smile. We are interested in noticing our entire experience.

It is fruitless to try to stop thinking or hearing, so instead we can learn to let thoughts and sounds arise and go without getting hooked by them. When we practice **it is helpful to learn to let go of all thoughts and sounds** (those we like as well as those we don't). It is easier to learn skills with something that is not emotionally charged.

Variation

Take out the "sounds" element of this practice and do it outside in a more informal way.

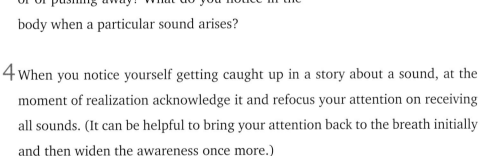

1 Take your seat and spend a few minutes **settling your attention on the breath and body** (see page 70).

2 When you are ready, **expand your attention to become aware of any sounds.** The sound of your breath entering and leaving the body may still be present, along with sounds from farther away. Your awareness is like a radar. There is no need to go hunting for sounds—simply allow yourself to receive any that come your way.

3 Experience any sound simply as a collection of notes at a particular pitch, tone and timbre. **Notice your own response:** is it one of liking or of pushing away? What do you notice in the body when a particular sound arises?

4 When you notice yourself getting caught up in a story about a sound, at the moment of realization acknowledge it and refocus your attention on receiving all sounds. (It can be helpful to bring your attention back to the breath initially and then widen the awareness once more.)

5 Continue in this way for 5 minutes or so.

6 When you feel ready, **let go of the sounds and allow your thoughts to take center stage.** What do you notice when you make this invitation? Often our thoughts become shy and scuttle off into the shadows!

7 We are practicing seeing our thoughts simply as passing events—like sounds that arise, becoming louder before they fade away. We may not like them, but we can't control them so we might as well acknowledge them since they are present anyway.

8 **We are not trying to stop thinking.** We are practicing not getting caught up in a particular thought story. Of course thoughts will occur, and when they do we acknowledge them as "thinking" and watch them arise, proliferate, and fade.

9 Some thoughts are "stickier" than others, but the instruction remains the same.

10 We can see our thoughts as:

- Passing clouds—some heavy and dark, others wispy, or soft and fluffy.

- Buses (a more urban image): imagine waiting at the bus stop and seeing buses ("thoughts") come and go, maybe singly or sometimes in groups. From time to time you may find you've jumped on a "thought" bus without being aware of it. If that happens, acknowledge it and just "jump off" again!

- Imagine yourself sitting in a movie theater or playhouse, with your thoughts being enacted on the stage or screen. Sometimes you may be totally wrapped up in what is unfolding—your heart pounding, your hands gripping the seat—but when you realize this, remind yourself that you are simply watching players on a stage

11 Remember that **you can use your breath as an anchor at any time.** Often it's useful after disengaging from a particular story to come back to a clear point of focus, such as the felt sense of breath.

LEARNING TAKES TIME

Be patient! Being with our thoughts in this way is always challenging. We've spent our lives chasing our thought stories, so learning a different way of being takes time and is difficult. It is important to acknowledge that if you find yourself judging your thinking mind.

12 When you are ready to finish, bring your attention back to the breath for a moment or two to conclude the practice.

CONVERSATION AS PRACTICE

Our brain is constantly receiving and interpreting information. However, the mood we are in affects the spin we put on our experience, and our thoughts will also affect the stories we tell ourselves.

When we are feeling down or stressed, we are more likely to focus only on evidence that supports a negative story, discarding any information that might disprove it. If our interpretation can be so easily skewed by our mood, how can we ensure that what we hear someone saying to us is what they really mean? *Conversation as Practice* is an opportunity to do just that.

A crucial part of this practice is *Listening Mindfully*, so it's helpful if you have become familiar with that first and have practiced the wider awareness of noticing what you are experiencing in the body as you listen (see page 46).

In *Conversation as Practice* we listen mindfully and at the same time maintain a wider awareness of what we are experiencing in the body. When the speaker has finished, we reflect back to them what we think they have said. We can use phrases such as:

"Can I just check I've understood you correctly ...?"
"So what you are saying is ... Is that right?"

It's important to create the opportunity for the speaker to correct any misunderstandings or misrepresentations on the part of the listener, and there may be a bit of mindful back and forth before the speaker is happy that what they have said has been understood as they intended.

Conversation as Practice can feel clunky at first. You may want to have a go with friends and family, or you can explore practicing it without anyone being aware you are doing so.

There are three parts to *Conversation as Practice*:

1 Listen mindfully.

2 Maintain awareness of your own felt experience in the body.

3 Reflect what you have heard and be willing to have it corrected.

Move back and forth between them, rather than tackling them sequentially.

REFLECT....

_____

_____

_____

_____

_____

_____

Life is made up of millions of fleeting experiences. It is your choice whether to sleep through them or wake up and live them.

EXPLORING THE WANTING CREATURE

The desire to have something, whether it is a second helping at dinner or the latest gadget, can be very powerful. I like to imagine it as a slumbering creature curled up contentedly until desire wakens it and it roars into being.

This is the perfect opportunity to explore what "wanting" really feels like. Where do we notice it in the body, what thoughts are we aware of, and are there any emotions present? What motivates and drives the Wanting Creature? How do we feel afterward if we allow the Wanting Creature to get its way? How long does the enjoyment last? What do we notice then in the head, heart, and body?

As always, the key word here is **curiosity!**

Exploring the Wanting Creature can happen on many different levels. For example, we often eat without awareness—reaching for that slice of cake or second helping while on autopilot. **The invitation here is to bring that moment of impulse into awareness:** to explore what it feels like in the body and notice any accompanying thoughts or emotions. Decide whether you are really hungry or whether the impulse might derive from boredom or something else. Be curious. You may still decide to have the cake or the second helping, but you will be choosing to do so intentionally.

If, after consideration, you decide to have the treat, eat it mindfully rather than allowing the experience to be tarnished by judging thoughts, guilt, and shame. If you eat it and notice that actually you already had enough and now you feel uncomfortably full, pay attention so that next time you can add that information to the decision-making process.

You can follow this process with many different moments of impulse: reaching for the next glass of wine, buying that top you don't really need, checking Facebook or Twitter, opening your email program … **Pay attention before, during, and after any actions that arise without clear intention.**

HALFWAY REVIEW

If you have been following the suggestions week by week, you will now have reached a point where it is worth reflecting on your experience—without judging it, but simply to gather information to guide you.

You may feel that you have not been as diligent as you intended at the start, but how often do things go exactly to plan? However your practice has been, there is benefit to be gained from taking stock of what you have noticed.

TRY THIS

Take some time to settle into Watching the Breath *(see page 26). When you feel ready, silently ask, "What am I learning?" Let the phrase go without any expectation of receiving something particular back. Repeat it every so often, tuning into your experience and noticing any resonance—there may be nothing or you may notice fragments of images or felt sensations. Just be open to whatever might arise. You can choose alternative phrases if you like, such as "What am I noticing?" or anything else that feels appropriate.*

Continue for at least 10 minutes, and conclude your practice by coming back to the breath for a moment or two.

When you have finished, use these pages to reflect on what came up for you. Perhaps begin by writing the phrase you used, for example—"What am I learning? I am learning …"—and then see what comes up. Write without editing or worrying about spelling or grammar; simply explore what came up for you.

Finally, write a sentence about how you would like to approach the next period of practice. **Is there anything you would like to do differently?**

SUFFERING CAN BE OPTIONAL

Pain, whether physical or psychological, is an unavoidable part of the human condition. We can't stop it arising. That is the first dart or arrow. Suffering, on the other hand—the second dart or arrow—is the result of our resistance to experiencing pain.

Our resistance can take the form of thoughts about the pain: "If this doesn't get better I'm not going to be able to go back to work … my sick leave is running out … my health insurance won't pay for more treatment … how will I meet the mortgage next month … I'll lose my home as well as my job," and so on. Such thoughts explode into a plethora of "what ifs" that create associated emotions such as fear, anger, and frustration as well as the physical sensations (clenched fists or jaw, cramps in the stomach, and so on) that are associated with those emotions. These are very unpleasant, and may lead to us experiencing thoughts about the unpleasant feelings themselves: "I shouldn't be feeling like this; I should be able to handle this; I'm such a loser that I'm feeling this way." And so the cycle continues.

Resistance may also take the form of tension around the discomfort—bracing oneself physically against our internal experience.

Acknowledging that we have the power to do something different can be liberating, since we often feel more stressed when things feel out of our control, but it can also be frightening. It can be easier to stay with what is familiar to us, however unpleasant. It can be easier to absolve ourselves of all responsibility about our experience and just give into it "because it's not my fault and there is nothing I can do." Unfortunately, this path is one of unnecessary suffering.

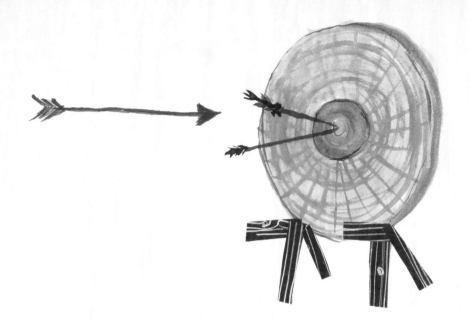

WHAT CAN WE DO?

- **We can learn to notice the particular song of repetitive emotions that is playing in our mind.** What is number one on today's hit parade? Acknowledging the story is essential.

- We can **bring humor to our experience**, to give us perspective, allowing us to become less caught up in it.

- We can use the skills learned through practicing *Mindfulness of Breath and Body* (see page 70) and **bring our attention to our breath as well as any physical sensations** arising out of the experience. When we bring our attention to a physical focus we let go of our thoughts (and we will have to do this repeatedly).

- **We can use the experience as an opportunity** to practice *Being with the Difficult* (see page 128).

Whatever we decide to do, it is important that we let go of any desire to make our experience better—to seek a particular outcome. We can't do anything about the physical pain, the grief, the loss, or whatever form the first dart takes; instead we are learning to be with it rather than resist it and so create additional suffering.

EXPLORING RESISTANCE

When we practice mindfulness we are interested in exploring ALL states of mind. Suffering arises because we want something to be different, and we don't like what we are experiencing in the present moment (this might be an internal or external experience).

Because that sense of "not liking," "not wanting," "resisting," and "pushing away" are all powerful emotions, they are often associated with strong physical sensations. The body braces itself against the resistance, tightening and tensing up. This felt sensation can give us an important early clue that we don't like something. Once we've been alerted that resistance is present, we can then widen our beam of awareness to include our thoughts and emotions.

This week, pay attention to moments when you are resisting your experience. It may be when you are on a crowded commuter train, sitting down to practice, eating something you dislike, or tackling a particular job you've been avoiding —we are rarely short of opportunities to face resistance!

Tune into the body. What do you notice?
Tune into your thinking. What do you notice?
Tune into your emotions. What do you notice?

It's important to approach this activity with an attitude of curiosity, and without judging what you notice. The resistance is present, so resisting the resistance is counterproductive. Instead, we want to move in closer to it, **approaching it with an attitude of friendly interest and without any hidden agenda of wanting it go away.**

Move in closer to the sense of avoidance. Where are you feeling it? Is it moving around or staying still? How would you describe the sensations? If you try not to experience it—if you suppress it or push it away—what happens?

You may want to pay particular attention to the out-breath, and perhaps repeat silently to yourself, "It's okay—let me feel it." By doing this you are not saying that whatever is happening is okay—sometimes it is not—but you are honoring your response to it, and how you are feeling. These sensations and emotions are present, even if we don't like them and wish they were not.

Make a note of your experience of resistance, avoidance, not liking, not wanting, pushing away ... How many different types can you identify? Notice whether different types of resistance create a different felt experience?

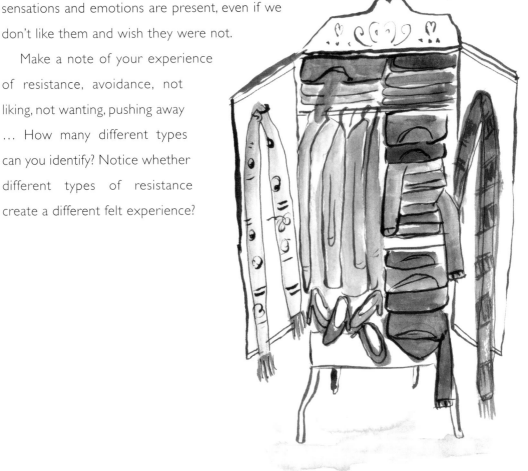

REFLECT.....

_____

_____

_____

_____

_____

_____

_____

_____

_____

_____

_____

_____

What we do in this moment will
influence what happens next.

BLUE SKY IS ALWAYS THERE

I was on retreat in north Wales. It had rained for several days and the cloud hung heavy, shrouding the mountains of Snowdonia. As I was doing walking practice outside I raised my eyes to the sky and the dark clouds parted. A bright blue streak of sky was visible for a moment before being covered by cloud once more. In that moment I was reminded that the sky is always blue, regardless of any weather that might obscure it temporarily. Can we see what happens to us as simply weather in our sky?

Describe the weather of your mood in this moment, right now, in words, pictures, images, or shapes. Don't think about it, just put down what comes to you in this moment, without trying to make sense of it.

Notice the language you are using and remember that weather is transient and ever-changing and so "low mood is here" is a more accurate "weather" description than "I am low" which feels fixed and permanent. Paying attention to the words you use can give helpful feedback. Experiment with how you describe your moods and notice how that makes you feel.

MOVING TOWARD ACCEPTANCE

For many people, "acceptance" implies giving up, a sense of resignation. Acceptance in mindfulness is different: it is deliberate and active, without the unconscious and passive quality of autopilot (see page 34).

Moving toward acceptance is about taking baby steps. In our mindfulness practice **the first step of acceptance is acknowledgment of what is** (sometimes that is all we can do). Many of us spend a lot of time and energy wishing things were different. Yet if we are not willing to acknowledge how things really are—even if we don't like them—how can we make an informed decision on what to do next? **We can determine what is best to do next only if we really know where we are.**

HOW WOULD IT FEEL IF WE STOPPED FIGHTING AGAINST OR RESISTING THE WAY THINGS REALLY ARE?

When we meditate, **we explore accepting what is by turning toward it,** bringing an attitude of curiosity and interest to the experience. We investigate whether it is possible to relate to it differently from usual. We practice this first on the small discomforts that commonly arise when we sit and meditate—the pins and needles or the itch on our nose—and gradually build up the skill and confidence to apply it when more challenging situations arise.

We can experiment with various options that can bring space to the experience:

1 We can breathe into the discomfort, imagining the breath entering and leaving the body in a narrow beam directed toward the uncomfortable sensation.

2 We can keep our attention focused on the breath in the torso (specifically the belly or the chest), but at the same time maintain an awareness of the discomfort. We breathe with it.

3 We can move in a little closer to the sensation to explore it in greater depth. What shape is it? Does it move around or is it constant and still? How would you describe it?

Whatever we choose to do, **it is important to let go of any expectation that the sensation will go away.** We are deliberately allowing the sensation to be experienced rather than resisting it or attempting to create an alternative. We are noticing how we relate to the unfolding experience, becoming aware, for example, if there is a tightening or tensing around the sensation, if we are bracing against it. If there is, we acknowledge it. It can be helpful to repeat silently "It's okay, it's okay, let me feel it."

In everyday life we are constantly judging our experience as good, bad, or neutral. If we can bring this pivotal moment into awareness, we can choose what we want to do next. **We can choose to move into approach rather than avoidance mode,** knowing that by doing so we are engaging the higher executive functions of the pre-frontal cortex rather than the more primitive areas of the brain, which are governed by fearful thinking. Which mode of operating do you think is more helpful in daily life?

Approach mode involves not gritting our teeth and bracing ourselves, but rather acknowledging how we are thinking and feeling emotionally and physically and breathing with it. We allow all that to be present in our experience as we observe it and our relationship to it.

The root of the word "acceptance" is to accept, that is to receive, so there is an element of consent or agreement. We often tune out of things we don't like, and get through as best we can. However, the attitude we bring to an activity can transform it. If we can experiment with deliberately engaging with the activity itself and how we relate to it, we may discover all kinds of things. Try it and see.

There are various opportunities in the activities to explore our own experience of resistance and its opposite, acceptance, as well as ways we can begin to relate differently to these states of mind.

WHAT DOES ACCEPTANCE MEAN FOR ME?

Acceptance can seem too much to ask sometimes, but we can explore what it means to us in terms of emotions and sensations and then play with the idea of acceptance in our practice.

Sit and take a few minutes to connect with the breath and the body (see page 70). Then bring to mind a time when you experienced acceptance. Perhaps you were accepted by another person, or perhaps you accepted a situation or a sensation. **Holding this memory in awareness, explore the felt sensations of the experience.** How would you describe them? What words or images come to mind? Just notice and observe, without judging what is arising. When you feel ready, record your experience in whatever way feels right for you— single words, descriptions, or pictures.

Sometimes when we do this we may notice the opposite of acceptance, resistance. That too is worthy of exploration (see page 116).

Does acceptance feel possible for you? You may want to write down some ideas about how you could explore introducing acceptance into your practice and everyday life.

COPING SPACE

*When things are difficult, we are not always able to do something like taking ourselves off for a walk or calling a friend. However, we can always do a **Breathing Space** (see page 88) with an extra step—a **Coping Space**.*

We introduced *The Breathing Space* in Week 20, and by now I hope you have had a chance to familiarize yourself with it and use it regularly. The *Coping Space* follows the same structure, but we introduce a self-soothing element to step 2. After acknowledging how you are feeling, bring your attention to your breathing and repeat silently to yourself "It's okay."

When we do this, we are not saying that the situation is okay—it may well not be—but rather **accepting that whatever we feel is okay.** It is our experience, even if we wish it weren't.

As well as repeating the words, you could place a hand on your chest or cross your arms paying attention to any points of contact. Practice the *Coping Space* any time this week when things feel a bit tricky. Practice it without any expectations.

WORKING WITH IMPULSES

Our actions are driven by our thoughts, feelings, and emotions, but we are usually unaware of them. We can break the cycle of reactivity by learning to bring the different threads that form our experience into awareness.

Sitting practice (see page 28) provides the perfect opportunity to work intentionally with an impulse. Notice how you end your practice. Do you stop abruptly, or is the close of your practice more measured and intentional? If the former is true, play with the "three strikes" suggestion by the meditation teacher Jack Kornfield:

- When you become aware of the impulse to end your practice, notice it. Become aware of **how the impulse manifests itself in the body**. What are you feeling physically? What thoughts are buzzing around your head—**what is driving the impulse?** Perhaps you notice a to-do list ticking off in your head … Notice this first impulse in all its manifestations.
- Before long, the impulse will probably arise again. That is strike 2. Once more, stay present with what is arising. Remind yourself **that you are practicing "staying" with a spirit of curiosity and gentleness.**
  - The third time the impulse arises, acknowledge it, but this time allow yourself to conclude your practice. Perhaps bring your attention to your breath for a moment or two or bring your hands together to end your practice.

START FROM WHERE YOU ARE

Many of us spend much of our time measuring our progress against an invisible yardstick. If we don't think we have lived up to this imaginary scale—and we rarely have—we berate ourselves for "not being good enough."

All too often we throw in the towel and abandon the task, saying that if we can't do something "perfectly" there is no point in doing it at all. Perhaps we don't join our friends for a run because we are "not fit enough"—and so we miss out on an opportunity to socialize while getting fitter; maybe we give up meditating because we haven't been doing it diligently every day, and so we don't discover the freedom of simply starting from where we are.

This week, notice the occasions when you don't start an activity, or when you abandon something because you don't think you are doing it well enough. Treat the thought "not good enough" as a red flag, which causes you to pause and question that thought. Who is setting this standard? Perhaps the task requires experiential learning and skill to be acquired over time. There is no way that things will change unless you are willing to have a go and acknowledge that it can be okay to be a "work in progress." Can something be "good enough," meaning that you have done your best considering all the extenuating circumstances?

Notice the thoughts that arise and pay particular attention to any physical sensations or emotions arising alongside them. You could take a *Breathing Space* (see page 88), making sure not to miss out the first step of acknowledging what is happening for you. When you move into the second stage, while you are breathing perhaps say silently to yourself "It's okay, it's okay."

BEING WITH THE DIFFICULT

How can we experience something difficult in a different way? For the "in-the-moment" times, when we may be at work or in another challenging situation and feel overwhelmed by what we are experiencing, informal practices like **Feet on the Floor** *(see page 30) or a* **Coping Space** *(see page 125) can be helpful.*

At other times we may want to bring an ongoing difficulty (whether a situation or physical pain) to our practice in a more formal way. On these occasions, the following practice or the *Self-compassion* practice on page 144 may be helpful.

To do this practice, find a time and place where you feel safe and will not be disturbed. Take as long as you need to settle yourself on your breath and body so you feel grounded (see *Mindfulness of Breath and Body*, page 70).

LEARN THE FOUNDATIONAL SKILLS

This practice can be challenging, so it is important that you have already become familiar with the skills learned by regularly practicing *Watching the Breath* (see page 26) and *Mindfulness of Breath and Body* (see page 70). Also, to begin with, experiment with bringing small difficulties to mind—irritation with a colleague at work, for example—rather than a big life event.

1 Notice where in the body you are feeling the breath most strongly, and **make a clear intention that this is the place to which you will bring your attention at any point in the practice when things feel tricky or you want to steady yourself.**

2 When you are ready, deliberately **invite whatever is preying on your mind to the forefront.**

3 Notice what arises when you do so, acknowledging the accompanying thoughts even if you feel they are inappropriate in some way.

4 It's important to be curious about your experience as a whole, perhaps asking yourself silently **"What is here?"** Stay open to whatever comes up, if anything, without any expectation.

5 As you notice what arises you can name particular emotions, for example, by saying "fear is here." **Repeatedly naming an emotion** has been shown to dampen its activity in the brain.

6 **Take a friendly interest in the felt sensations of the**

experience. What are you feeling physically in the body, and where? How would you describe it—sharp, stabbing, tingling …—and what characteristics does it have—solid, soft? Is it constant, intermittent, unchanging, or moving?

7 You can use the breath to help by directing it into the specific location of the pain or strong sensation. Alternatively, focus your attention on the breath in the torso while holding the pain or sensation in awareness and breathing with it.

It's important to take baby steps with this practice. You may "be" with the experience for only a second or two before retreating to the breath to anchor yourself, before returning to the experience for another few seconds. **It is wise to take this practice slowly, using the breath to steady yourself throughout, rather than jumping straight in and becoming overwhelmed.**

It's very easy to fall into "fixing mode" with this practice, hoping the "difficulty" will go away or trying to make it do so. It's very important that we remind ourselves that this practice is about turning toward our pain or difficulty, rather than avoiding it. Avoidance activates our internal threat mechanisms and keeps us locked in a cycle of suffering, whereas an approach mode helps us to be with it.

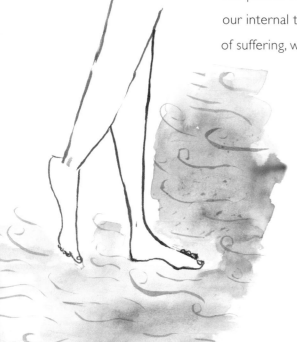

REFLECT....

_____

_____

_____

_____

_____

_____

TAKING A MINDFUL MINUTE

We can all find 60 seconds in our day and Michael Chaskalson, the author of Mindfulness in Eight Weeks *(2014), has turned this into a simple practice. It's a helpful way to bring us back to the body and focus—just for 1 minute—on our breathing. I'd encourage you to do this practice as often as you can, helping yourself to remember by using a prompt of some kind, perhaps a particular photograph or a word on a sticky note on your desk. Some people put colored dot stickers on computers or telephones as a prompt to take a minute when they notice it.*

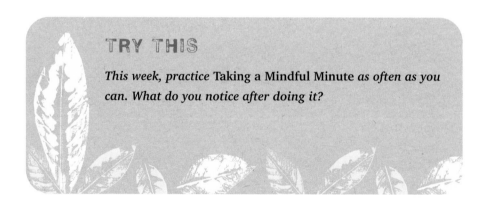

TRY THIS

This week, practice Taking a Mindful Minute *as often as you can. What do you notice after doing it?*

For this practice, we will count the number of breaths we take in a minute. One breath consists of a complete in-breath and a complete out-breath. You will need a timer of some kind. Most cellphones have one, or you could use an old-fashioned egg timer or kitchen minute minder. Set the equipment up for 60 seconds so that it will need just a simple push of a button to start. Begin by taking some time to settle into your breathing. Then, on your next in-breath, start timing and begin counting your breaths.

Breathing in ... breathing out ... One.
Breathing in ... breathing out ... Two.
Continue until the timer goes off.

How many breaths did you count? Write that number down here.

_____

The number of breaths you take is irrelevant. I have done it with a group that varied from nine to twenty breaths, but there is no right or wrong. We are simply creating a number for each individual to use in the future.

REFLECT....

_____

_____

_____

_____

_____

_____

The present moment is the only moment we have a choice: how will you respond?

EXPLORING ALTERNATE VIEWPOINTS

In the film Dead Poets Society (1989) the teacher John Keating, played by the late Robin Williams, tells his students to stand on top of their desks to see the world differently. How often do we do this? We can become very attached to our own particular viewpoint (often with ourselves at the center), but if we look at things differently all kinds of possibilities open up.

This week the invitation is to explore the theme of alternative viewpoints.

Physically choose a different perspective. For example, when we are feeling overwhelmed, it can be helpful to look out of a window, find an open space, climb a hill, or go to the top of a building. Engaging with the wider world encourages us to look outward rather than get caught up in an internal struggle. We can use the environment to support and strengthen our internal state of mind.

Explore viewpoints in relationships. We can become irritated when something doesn't go our way, but if we can pause, take a step back, and see it from a wider perspective we may notice that what is occurring isn't personal, but is down to a host of other things. Or perhaps there are just different options, rather than a right way and a wrong way. Our interpretation of an event is influenced by what comes immediately before it, our

MEDITATING REGULARLY

As we have seen, before and after brain scans of novice meditators showed that regular practice led to increased activity in the temporoparietal junction, the area concerned with perspective, compassion, and empathy (see page 81).

mood, and our thoughts, and the last two may influence each other. Our thoughts and moods affect how we feel physically in the body, and these felt sensations affect our thoughts and moods. This constant cycle can work against us, or we can harness the knowledge it provides. How many different viewpoints can you come up with to a particular situation that is current for you?

Project ourselves into another person's viewpoint. This could be someone who is very different from you, perhaps someone from whom you would normally shy away or whom you might judge. In their shoes, how would you feel, react, and behave? Be honest!

Open your eyes and explore new perspectives.

THOUGHTS

Meditation can help us see our thoughts as passing mental events, rather like weather fronts. When we meditate, we begin to notice our thoughts coming and going. We can begin to see how they are influenced by our state of mind and how they can in turn maintain and feed a particular state of mind.

When we feel down or stressed we are more likely to interpret things negatively. That negativity can make us feel vulnerable and anxious, keeping us in a state of hyper-vigilance and maintaining the body's state of alert, which in turn prompts the continued release of the stress hormone cortisol, which can keep us stuck in this cycle (see page 92).

Anxiety is created by fear of something happening, and that "something" is caused by the story we tell ourselves. If we can see it simply as a story rather than as fact, such thoughts lose their emotional charge. Notice your habitual thought patterns and, without judging them, which you are particularly prone to. Acknowledge them, notice how you can easily get hooked into them, and, most importantly, be curious about how they manifest themselves in the body. Common unhelpful thought patterns include:

CATASTROPHIZING
Making things out to be worse than they are.

It can be helpful to notice the type of language we are using to describe our experience and modify it since catastrophizing thoughts and words cause anxiety to escalate.

OVER-GENERALIZING
Turning one example of an experience into something that "always" happens to you.

It can be helpful to remind ourselves to employ "beginner's mind" (see page 21) and be open to the possibilities arising in each moment.

MIND-READING
Assuming we know what another person is thinking.

It can be helpful to challenge our assumption and remind ourselves to stick with what we know to be fact.

BLACK-AND-WHITE THINKING
Being overly judgmental and believing things are either right or wrong, or good or bad.

It is easy to ignore all the shades of gray that can make up our experiences. This type of all-or-nothing thinking is common in perfectionists, who believe that anything less than the best is a failure. Meditating regularly gives a wider perspective.

CRYSTAL-BALL GAZING
Believing we know what will happen in the future (and often assuming the worst).

We can remind ourselves that the future is determined by what happens in the present moment, and that that is the only moment in which we have the power to do something different.

FOCUSING ON THE NEGATIVE
When we are feeling down we are more likely to focus on anything negative that supports the way we are feeling.

We will even ignore evidence contrary to the story that we are telling ourselves.

NOTICING THE JUDGING MIND

We are all constantly judging ourselves and others to see where we fit within our particular "tribe."

Sometimes our tribe may be our nationality, sometimes it's our neighborhood or group of friends, or maybe just our family. We can be part of a multitude of different groups at any one time. We are also always judging our experience—as good, bad, or neutral—and how we respond to the experience is often determined by that moment of interpretation.

This week, pay attention to the judging mind. Notice that moment when you pass someone in the street and a judgment pops up in your mind. **There is no need to judge the judging, simply acknowledge it and notice any associated thoughts or emotions.**

If the judging mind is active when you are with somebody, take it as a helpful warning that your opinions may be biased.

When we judge someone, we lock on to a particular way of interpreting them or their behavior. The judgment may be based on information that is out of date or perhaps not even true, but simply something we have read or heard about at second hand. The danger is that we close down and become blind to the myriad possibilities that might arise if we could remain **open and curious.**

To begin with, simply pay attention, and acknowledge when the judging mind is present. Then as you become more used to doing this, you can start to bring your attention to the judging. Notice what you are experiencing in the body, and any emotions, and breathe into them. Be curious about the judging and the judged.

REFLECT....

_____

_____

_____

_____

_____

_____

ZONING OUT

When we are tired we often zone out with activities that take us away from what we are experiencing. These can take the form of excessive alcohol or drugs, or perhaps hours of mindless television.

Apart from the physical dangers of long-term substance misuse, any activity that stops us feeling is shutting us off from living life, with all that it entails. **Experiencing emotions—even the unpleasant ones—makes us feel alive.** The occasional binge on never-ending reruns of a made-for-television soap when we are tired will not do lasting harm, but if we repeatedly shut down when things are uncomfortable the behavior becomes habitual, and so we shut down from all the positive experiences, too. Life becomes joyless and we feel as if we are simply existing, drifting through it with no purpose or meaning.

It's easy to slide into unhelpful patterns without realizing, so pay attention this week to those occasions when you feel you are turning away from your experience and choosing to zone out. Pay attention to what prompts and drives this behavior. **Can you do something different? How do you feel once you have?**

Sometimes small shifts are all that is needed. Turning the television off when your favorite show has finished, rather than moving on to the next thing without making a conscious choice, is a good start.

REFLECT....

_____

_____

_____

_____

_____

_____

SELF-COMPASSION

Research suggests that regularly practicing mindfulness meditation increases compassion and empathy. However, we can also choose to do a practice that cultivates compassion, specifically compassion for oneself. Many of us struggle to show the same kindness toward ourselves that, without hesitation, we would demonstrate to a friend or loved one who was suffering. Introducing a self-compassion meditation into our regular practice can help to redress this balance.

For this practice, take your time to settle into the *Mindfulness of Breath and Body* (see page 70), beginning to tune into the breath and paying attention to the length of each in-breath and each out-breath.

If you like, you can place a hand over your heart, chest, or belly, or perhaps hold both arms lightly. Find any place where you would like to connect with a felt sense of the body in this moment.

Then choose two of the words and phrases shown in the word cloud opposite—or others of your own—and repeat one on the in-breath and the other on the out-breath.

Keep repeating the words, letting them drop like pebbles into water and noticing any ripples in your

experience. Stay in tune with the breath and repeat your chosen word(s) over and over. Allow yourself to receive these words.

As you become more familiar with this practice, you can experiment with saying certain words as you breathe in and others when you breathe out. Or you might want to repeat the words only on the out-breath. Explore and be curious about what you notice.

Remember, there is no expectation of feeling anything particular, and especially not "warm and fuzzy" feelings! We are using the words or phrases to focus our attention, planting seeds of intention. We are opening our minds to the possibility that we may experience a moment of calm, peace, love, or whatever the word or phrase signifies. Our life may feel chaotic and difficult, but in this one moment it is possible to feel calm, strong, or whatever quality we have chosen. We are focusing only on this single moment at any one time.

WHAT NOURISHES ME: AN ACTION PLAN

When we become too busy or stressed, the first things to go are often what are seen as "optional extras," the things we do for pleasure: the foreign-language evening class, choir practice, meeting up with friends for a drink, going to the gym …

Before we know it, our life revolves around work or perhaps caring for a sick or elderly relative and we are not doing anything to nourish our mental and physical well-being. As our world becomes narrower and narrower, we are at risk of burnout and we feel drained and exhausted.

What nourishes you? Make a list of anything that makes you feel good, whether it has a physical, emotional, or mental benefit. Some things might seem quite small—taking a long, hot bath or calling a friend for a chat—while others may need a bit of planning. Some activities might involve a challenge, but leave you with a sense of achievement. Some may be things you've done in the past and let go, others may be things you've only dreamed of; it doesn't matter—just put down as much as you can without editing.

Now make an action plan. Can you do one of these activities at least once this week? Can you set in motion plans for one of the things that requires more organization? Set realistic goals and begin with things that feel achievable. Take baby steps towards ones that are more complex and perhaps require some preparation.

ACTION PLAN

ACTIVITY	BY	DONE

Involve friends and family if you need to in order to help you implement your plan.

Remember, if we look after ourselves we will be better able to take care of those who rely on us.

NO ONE ELSE HAS THE ANSWER

One of my favorite poems by the Chinese philosopher Lao Tzu begins with the words "Always we hope someone else has the answer" before going on to say "This is it. No one else has the answer." It's easy to absolve ourselves of responsibility for what happens to us, but—while sometimes things do happen through no fault of our own— there is plenty about our experience that we can influence. And of course we can always choose how we relate to those things that we can't control.

When we begin to pay attention to our experience in mindfulness practice, we start to see how much suffering we create for ourselves. We notice the stories we create about why this happened or that did not. At the same time, through regular meditation we connect with the inner strength and wisdom that we all have but sometimes lose sight of. Lao Tzu's poem continues: "At the center of your being you have the answer; you know who you are and you know what you want."

One of the benefits of mindfulness is that it is something we can explore at any time and in any place. We don't need props or professional help (although both can be helpful from time to time), but we simply pay attention to our experience in a particular way and use our breath and other physical sensations to anchor ourselves to the present.

Paying attention to bodily sensations can give us invaluable feedback about a situation and how we really feel about it, rather than how we think we should feel.

We always have our breath to turn to, and the more regularly we do so the stronger an anchor it becomes.

This week, notice those moments when your default is to put the responsibility of your experience on to someone else, and instead do something different. Take ownership of it and acknowledge that there are small actions we can take in any situation. Taking control, albeit in a small way, is empowering.

You might want to look at what you are eating or drinking (or not), the activities you are taking part in, your sleep patterns, and your other habits. Is there something you could do differently?

You might want deliberately to bring a situation that is on your mind to your sitting practice. After a period of settling on the breath and body, silently ask yourself a key question or two and notice your response. Keep repeating the question, and remain open to whatever comes up, rather than looking for a particular outcome.

REFLECT....

_____

_____

_____

_____

_____

_____

THE IMPORTANCE
OF INTENTION

Intention is the root of our motivation. The desire to practice mindfulness meditation must come from within; it's not something you can do because someone has told you to.

People are often drawn to mindfulness at a time of change, perhaps an illness or momentous change in their home or work life that has shaken things up. Such events can make us aware that it is important to do something different.

It is important to understand why you are doing this, what brings you to the "mat" each time. Your vision will probably align with the values that guide the way you live: the choices you make, the type of parent you are, the way you treat your colleagues, and so on.

Practicing mindfulness regularly requires time, and it is likely that you will have to make time to fit it in. That will mean giving something up—perhaps an extra 10 minutes in bed or a television show. **You can give something up only if you value what is taking its place.**

It is also important to update this periodically by checking in with yourself and reconnecting with your commitment to practice. Throughout this book there are opportunities for you to do so, and, of course, it is something you can reflect on at any time.

As well as exploring the intention that underlies our practice, **we can pay attention to the intention that underlies our actions.** When we say something or behave in a particular way, what is our intention? Is it to undermine someone or score a point, or are we acting out of goodwill, generosity, and kindness? The same words spoken with either of those intentions will be received very differently.

NAMING WHAT IS PRESENT

The unmentionable can be given greater power than it deserves by becoming "that which must not be named," something hidden and secret that inspires fear.

Naming what is present for us is a common practice in meditation; by doing it we become familiar with a wide range of experiences and may notice connections between emotions, sensations, thoughts, and situations.

Stating that "anxiety is present" is acknowledging what is arising in our present moment. In this form it is also acknowledgment without over-identification. "I am anxious" suggests that it is a permanent state of affairs and part of who we are; "anxiety is present" has a transient quality, reminding us that it will pass in time.

We can practice naming when we sit and meditate. We do this with a very light touch—there's no need to search for the "perfect" word and it's important not to judge it or expect the feeling to disappear. Once it is named, we might also become aware of its physical manifestation in the body and any accompanying thoughts.

WHAT STOPS YOU PRACTICING?

Meditating for even 10 minutes a day can make a huge difference to how we feel. All the skills we learn "on the mat" are transferable to everyday life, and yet, even though we know practice is helpful, there will always be times when we find it a struggle.

It is usual for practice to go through ups and downs. For the beginner, just knowing that everyone struggles can be helpful; it is also useful to make that struggle an opportunity for practice.

Are you aware of a moment when you make the choice whether to meditate or not? What is the story you tell yourself? What do you notice in the body? Are there any emotions present? **Explore your resistance to practicing in the head, heart, and body.** If you let go of any judgments about not doing it, can you allow that resistance to be present? Can you acknowledge that it is there?

Experiment with what feels achievable. Take a few minutes to sit and ground yourself, and then ask yourself "Can I sit for 40 minutes?" (Start with a big number, since that is more likely to spark a response in the mind and body.) Notice what comes up. Then ask "Can I sit for 30 minutes?" Notice what comes up. Continue in this way, reducing the number and maintaining a sense of curiosity and playfulness. When you reach a number that feels right, your body will tell you. It may be only one minute, and that's okay. Simply start where you are.

Most people try to squeeze their practice into an already crowded day, but most quickly realize that they have to make time to practice. Acknowledging that this is important and that we need to make it a priority will make a difference.

REFLECT....

_____

_____

_____

_____

_____

_____

THE MOUNTAIN

Nature has a lot to teach us, and spending time outside is an excellent way to reconnect with the cycles of the seasons and the changing weather. We can also borrow images from nature to bring into our sitting practice; the mountain is always a popular one.

When you think of a mountain, what comes to mind? Think of some words that occur to you. They might have to do with how a mountain makes you feel, how you would describe it, or the characteristics of a mountain … or if you prefer, simply draw any images or shapes that come to mind.

1 Begin by spending some time *Watching the Breath* (see page 26). Pay particular attention to your posture: make sure the lower half of the body feels grounded, the torso rises out of the pelvis, and the crown of the head lifts toward the sky.

2 Now, bring to mind an image of a mountain. It may be a familiar one or a generic image, or one from a photograph or movie. Notice its shape and how it corresponds to your sitting position—the wider lower half connected to the ground, the shoulders and arms the slopes, and the head the mountain peak.

3 From the summit it is possible to see far and wide, with a 360-degree view. As we connect to the vastness of the sky above and the land unfolding below, we are reminded that there is a bigger world out there than our own.

4 Remind yourself of a mountain's qualities, its stability and strength regardless of the changing weather that assails it. The contours of the mountain may become weathered over time, but its essential nature remains unchanged. Can we simply sit with ourselves and honor our own surface appearance as we become weathered by time and experience? Can we sit with the shifting weather patterns of our mood, and instead of taking them personally simply see them as an integral part of being human? Can we borrow the qualities of the mountain and use them to support our practice?

5 Sit like a mountain. Hold whatever comes your way in awareness.

6 Continue in this way as long as you would like to. When you notice the impulse to stop, explore riding out the impulse a time or two before making the intention to conclude the practice.

A TYPICAL DAY

Make a list below of everything you do in a typical day. If every day is different, just do your best. List every activity you do from the moment you wake up until you go to bed. Try to break big activities down into smaller tasks and elements.

Key: Nourishing = **N**; Draining = **D**

Once you have listed your activities, decide whether you find an activity "nourishing" (N) or "draining" (D), or any other observation.

N   D   Other

_____ ☐ ☐ ☐

_____ ☐ ☐ ☐

_____ ☐ ☐ ☐

_____ ☐ ☐ ☐

_____ ☐ ☐ ☐

_____ ☐ ☐ ☐

What do you notice about your list? Are there any surprises?

Have another look at your list. Is it possible to turn any of your "draining" activities into neutral or even "nourishing" ones? Perhaps choose one to experiment with at first. **Make a note of what you discover.** Are there items on your list that you don't particularly enjoy but that do give you a sense of satisfaction? These "mastery" type of activities are often things you might put off such as cleaning the fridge, tidying up a closet, completing a tax return, sorting out out clothes to get rid of. Because completing these type of activities make us feel good, they are ones to do when you are feeling down. However, do make sure you break them down into achievable chunks otherwise they might feel overwhelming.

Remember that whether you choose a nourishing or mastery activity to do, it's important to do it without any expectation that it will make you feel a particular way. Practice "beginner's mind", viewing it as an experiment and do it for its own sake.

THE WAY WE DO AN ACTIVITY CAN DETERMINE HOW IT MAKES US FEEL

- If we don't like something, we often zone out from it or resist it, going into avoidance mode rather than approach mode. What happens if we pay attention instead?

When we are interested in something, we start noticing all kinds of things. Instead of resisting it, we turn toward it. Try it and see.

- Some activities in life may be unavoidable and quite challenging. In these instances, experiment with taking a moment to do a *Breathing Space* (see page 88) before and after, and even during. Perhaps make a conscious effort to do something restorative afterward. What would be helpful?

- Look for the "dead" spaces in your day: walking down a corridor, going to a different floor, holding on the phone …

All these can become opportunities to practice mindfulness, and all are a chance for us to connect with our breath and the present moment.

TAKING CARE OF OURSELVES

Sometimes we feel helpless when things are difficult. At moments like this, it can be helpful to do a Coping Space (see page 125) and add an action step.

After honestly acknowledging the reality of a situation and how we feel about it, we may realize that we can't fix it or make it better. In these situations, we can add a final step, asking **"What would be the most helpful for me to do now?' or 'How can I best take care of myself?'** This could be something that you find nourishing and pleasurable, or perhaps something that will give you a sense of satisfaction—it could even be doing some mindfulness practice.

Have a look at the list you made on pages 158–9 of Nourishing Activities and Mastery Activities. Draw on this list whenever you need to; it may be helpful to stick it on your fridge door or somewhere else where it will catch your eye and remind you to take care of yourself.

Practice the *Coping Space* whenever things feel difficult.

REFLECT....

_____

_____

_____

_____

_____

_____

PRACTICING KINDNESS TO ONESELF

Most of us give ourselves a hard time. We judge the way we look, the way we behave, and what we achieve, and all too often we fall short in our own mind. We practice a meanness to ourselves that goes far beyond the way we would treat a friend. The following activity is similar to that developed by Kristin Neff and Christopher Germer for their Mindful Self-compassion program.

We all have facets that we don't like about ourselves, or can recall times when we wish we'd done something differently. Bring to mind something about yourself that you're not happy about; it might be a personal trait, something about your appearance, or perhaps a time you could have behaved better. **Notice the words and phrases that form your thoughts when you bring it to mind, and write them down here.** When you hear these words addressed to yourself, how do they make you feel?

Then imagine your best friend had come to you with this same problem. You want to support them through a difficult time. What would you say to them? What words and phrases would you use? Imagine you were writing a letter to them now. When you have finished, set it aside for a few days before coming back to it and reading it as if it were addressed to you. How does it makes you feel? How is this different from the way you talked to yourself at the start of the practice? Which is more helpful?

REFLECT....

_____

_____

_____

_____

_____

_____

BEING WITH THOUGHTS

Thoughts are the cause of much of our unhappiness, because we believe them and take them at face value. However, once we begin to see them simply as mental events that are influenced by our mood, we can begin to get a better perspective. One way to do this is by writing down the different types of thought pattern we notice as we pay attention to our experience (see page 138).

Typical unhelpful thought patterns include:

OVER-GENERALIZING
MIND-READING
ALL-OR-NOTHING THINKING
FUTURE THINKING OR CRYSTAL-BALL GAZING
FOCUSING ON THE NEGATIVE
BLAMING SELF
BLAMING OTHERS
JUDGMENTAL—TOWARD SELF
JUDGMENTAL—TOWARD OTHERS

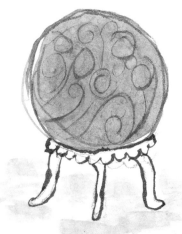

This list isn't exhaustive, of course—can you identify any others? Just make a note of the type of thought you are experiencing, rather than focusing too much on the content. Do you notice links between moods and particular types of thought? You don't need to do anything with what you notice; just write it down.

Words and phrases to look out for include "What if …," "I should …," "I must …," "I ought …," "I always …," "This always happens to me …," as these can act as cues that we are moving into unhelpful areas of thinking. Can you identify particular words and phrases that you commonly use with different types of thinking? As we begin to become aware of them, we can use these words and phrases as red flags to warn us that we are moving into unsafe waters. When we notice, we can take a *Breathing Space* (see page 88).

Type of thought pattern	Typical words and phrases I use	Mood I am in when experiencing these thoughts

TRANSFERABLE SKILLS

We can practice watching our thoughts in formal meditation practice (see pages 16, 26, 40, 70, 102, 128, and 156), and the skills we learn there are particularly helpful when we want to notice thoughts arising in our everyday life.

Remember that it's important not to beat yourself up over whatever you notice. The idea here is simply to notice what tracks your thoughts regularly run: when you bring them into awareness, that witnessing is the first stage of stepping back from them. The intention is to watch them rather than become caught up in them. When we observe our thoughts, we notice how they are influenced by our moods, and because of that they cannot be taken as fact. We begin to see that it is possible to liberate ourselves from the tyranny of our thoughts.

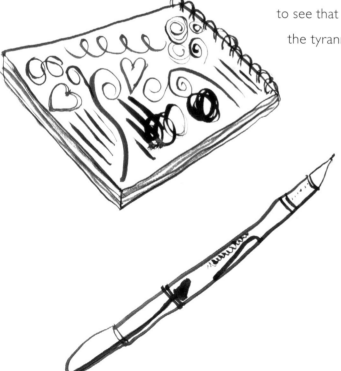

NO MAN IS AN ISLAND

The sixteenth-century poet John Donne's words are true for all of us. We are all part of a wider group, and often unhappiness is caused when, for whatever reason, we feel isolated from that group. Deliberately connecting with others can help to reduce this sense of disconnection, and we can do that by reaching out to strangers as well as people we already know.

We can connect with others through very simple gestures, such as looking them directly in the eye, smiling, shaking hands positively, holding a door open, offering a seat, giving directions to someone who is lost, and in many other ways. When we connect with someone—particularly a stranger, whom we could easily ignore as we drift along on autopilot—we bring ourselves into the present. At that moment of exchange there is a connection: we have noticed them, and they have noticed us.

When we do something positive for someone else we make ourselves feel good as well as them. They will feel that someone has noticed them, which means they matter, they are seen. In that moment they are not alone.

We can begin with people with whom we interact throughout our day: the barista handing us a drink, the bus driver taking our fare, the store assistant handing us our goods.

Experiment with this and reflect on what you notice.

REFLECT....

_____

_____

_____

_____

_____

_____

_____

_____

_____

_____

_____

_____

The intention that underlies our words
and actions invluences them and therefore
the outcome.

MAKING THE PRACTICE YOUR OWN

There are lots of different ways to practice mindfulness: formal practices that include sitting or movement meditations, and informal practices in which we pay attention to our everyday experience in a particular way. Most people prefer certain practices over others, and we might also be constrained by family or work commitments.

Sometimes we find certain practices helpful when we are in a particular frame of mind. For example, walking or another movement practice can help to settle a restless mind when sitting may be too challenging. When we are lying awake at night, unable to sleep, a simple *Body Scan* (see page 17) might be helpful.

It's worth reviewing the list of practices on pages 186 and marking those that have resonated particularly with you. You may also want to revisit the list of activities (see pages 186–187) and perhaps repeat those that were particularly helpful.

It can also be worthwhile to pay attention to the practices we resist. Be curious about that resistance and perhaps experiment with the practices from time to time, noticing how your attitude may change.

Once you have a sense of the practices and/or activities you find particularly helpful, make a note of them here with any observations from your experience that you think will be useful. Use this list to structure your day-to-day practice—both formally and informally—always keeping a light, flexible touch.

REFLECT....

_____

_____

_____

_____

_____

_____

MOVING WITH AWARENESS

Tuning into our physical experience is a great way to move ourselves out of the head, with all its future and past thinking, and bring us right into the present. It's also a good opportunity to integrate our mindfulness practice into every day, when we often move from one task to another: doing the household chores, going to pick the kids up from school, moving from one office to another, or even simply going to the kitchen or the bathroom.

The invitation this week is to pay attention regularly to the body in movement, in whatever form that takes (see *Mindful Movement*, page 40).

Experiment with that beam of awareness, sometimes keeping your focus tightly on physical sensations, for example, in the soles of the feet, and at other times widening it to include the whole body and perhaps the environment (a breeze on the cheek, the sun on your face, the sound of the traffic or birds singing …).

Moving with awareness may mean moving just one part of the body, particularly if your movement is limited for a physical reason. Our sense of touch can be acute: notice what you feel when you slowly rub your index finger against your thumb, for example.

Experiment with moving very slowly (perhaps somewhere private!); at other times, move at your normal pace. See how one or the other affects your attention.

Pay attention to what arises when you move in this way. Do you feel impatient or frustrated if you are moving slower than normal? Can you stay with sensations like this, noticing how a particular emotion manifests itself physically in the body and reminding yourself that, at this moment, you are simply moving without any particular goal?

Any physical exercise you might do—either on your own or as part of a class—represents an opportunity to introduce some mindfulness. Simply pay attention to your experience as it unfolds, without judging it—and let go of striving toward any particular goal.

Make a list of opportunities of introducing movement practice into your everyday life, and choose one to focus on one day. The next day add another, and so on.

visiting a friend · VACUUMING · tidying up · WALKING TO THE BATHROOM · putting on makeup · getting dressed · swimming · DUSTING · preparing food · making a drink · cycling · sweeping up · walking the dog · watering the plants · GOING TO THE STORE · LOADING THE DISHWASHER · going to the car

WHAT DOES BEING CENTERED FEEL LIKE?

Being centered suggests calm. Although we often associate calm people with an absence of strong emotion, there is also an element of balance; when we are calm we take things in our stride. When we are calm the seesaw of highs and lows is level, and if it ever begins to tip one way or another it returns easily to the point of balance. To maintain that balance may require constant small adjustments one way or another, so being balanced or calm is an active state that we have to participate in and perhaps deliberately move toward.

What does feeling centered mean for you? How do you feel when you are calm? You can explore this by paying attention to those moments when you do feel centered. What images come to mind? How do you feel physically? What emotions and thoughts do you notice, if any? Make a note of what you discover, and by doing so acknowledge and get to know this helpful state.

Think about whether there are particular activities that help to bring you into a place of calm. Those that have an element of focusing on the body

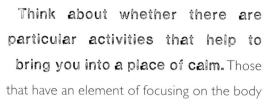

can be helpful; physical activities, like sport, but also those that emphasize creation through art, craft, cooking, or gardening. Activities that have a nurturing element—perhaps planting seeds or growing herbs or flowers—draw us closer to nature's cycles and the lessons they can teach us.

Perhaps being with certain people helps to center you. If so, who are they?

Noticing how we respond to different activities and people can help us to create an action list that we can turn to when necessary.

REFLECT....

_____

_____

_____

_____

_____

_____

It is better to practice a little and often than occasionally for long periods.

EMAIL AS PRACTICE

Email is now such an integral part of our lives that it's a great activity to use as "practice." Whether personal or work-related, an email is a message from another person, which lands in our personal space without warning. This may be a pleasant surprise if it's someone we want to hear from, but less welcome messages can tip us into a difficult place. And, of course, some emails are just routine and don't affect us either way.

Using email as practice is an opportunity for us to pay close attention to those sensations of liking, not liking, and being neutral. Once we have brought that moment of interpretation into awareness, we are more likely to be able to choose how we respond and so affect what happens what next. This is helpful in terms of our

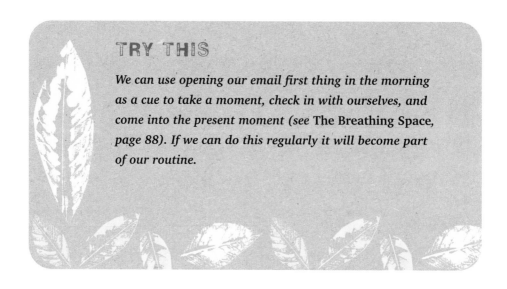

TRY THIS

*We can use opening our email first thing in the morning as a cue to take a moment, check in with ourselves, and come into the present moment (see **The Breathing Space**, page 88). If we can do this regularly it will become part of our routine.*

relationship with the senders of the email, but also has a wider benefit in terms of our practice in general, as it is an opportunity to practice being with and responding to a range of emotions.

When you look at those unread emails in your inbox, with different subjects and senders, notice how you are responding. Is it with a lift of the heart or a smile, or perhaps a clenching in the stomach and a tightening of the shoulders? Ask yourself what is happening in the body, and what you are noticing in terms of thoughts and emotions. Naming what is present can be helpful, as can keeping the attention on the breath and the feet on the floor if you notice a strong response.

Notice how you interpret particular emails. **Staying in the present moment can help to ground us and remind us that our interpretation is influenced by our frame of mind,** so if we are feeling stressed or down we are more likely to interpret something negatively (and vice versa, if we are feeling happy). If you notice a particularly negative train of thought with a harsh, judgmental tone, that's a red flag, reminding you to step back and ask yourself whether your response is appropriate.

Use body awareness as a cue so that you become aware of your posture. For example, you might be hammering out a reply. Notice, then pause. If you can, type a reply and keep it in draft form until you have a chance to re-read it in a more positive frame of mind.

It can be helpful to remind ourselves that people often write emails on the move, not necessarily taking care with words or phrases and often not reading things back before sending. Different nationalities also follow different email etiquette. Consequently, the content might be read very differently from the way the sender intended. This is also important to remember when you are sending or reading emails on your phone or tablet, or when you are writing to people of different nationalities.

Make a note of what you discover.

THE POWER OF SILENCE

How often do you explore silence? How frequently do you turn off the radio and the television, take some time out on your own and be with yourself without any distraction? We are often nervous of silence, as there is nowhere to hide: when we practice a period of silence and forgo checking emails and social media, chatting to friends, and even reading a book or newspaper, we inevitably come up against ourselves. Going on retreat is a traditional way to experience an extended period of practice and silence, but if that isn't possible, you can create your own silent retreat at home.

Choose a specific period of time; this will vary according to your circumstances. Perhaps experiment with a couple of hours initially, or half a day.

Plan your time so that you know what you are going to do next. A retreat is never just one long sitting practice, but instead is broken up into shorter periods of practice, including regular movement such as walking practice, yoga, or qi qong.

Collect guided practices from different teachers to bring some variety into the mix (CDs or downloads are a good place to start). As well as including the traditional sitting practices, you could try a *Mountain* meditation (see page 156) or a *Self-compassion* practice (see page 144) as well as lying-down practices such as a *Body Scan* (see page 17). Make sure always to include some movement between periods of sitting.

Also include some eating practice if you can. Prepare food that is particularly fresh and tasty (see page 56)

You may find journaling helpful, too. Use it to reflect on the practices, and perhaps also explore some of the writing practices in this book (see pages 12, 74, 182, and 184).

An extended period of meditation helps to deepen our practice. As always, we are not looking for a particular experience or to create a certain state of mind. It is rather an opportunity to notice how the weather of moods can vary from hour to hour, and even minute by minute. It may be challenging at times, so it can be helpful to remind ourselves that we don't have to enjoy it. Simply let the time unfold and explore what arises.

Don't forget to turn off and unplug your cellphone, and whatever you do, refrain from posting meditation selfies!

WRITING AS PRACTICE: EXPLORING INTENTION 3

Throughout the past weeks we have from time to time explored why we are doing this, and what brings us here. Week 51 presents another opportunity to connect with what you are learning and why you are doing it.

Writing as practice can be a good way of exploring what lies beneath our practice. It can be helpful to begin with a period of sitting practice, perhaps just *Watching the Breath* (see page 26).

When you are ready, set your phone timer or a kitchen timer for 3–5 minutes.

There are just three rules:

1 Don't stop. Any time you hesitate or don't know what to write, just repeat the words given opposite.

2 Don't edit your words or cross anything out. There is no need to worry about handwriting, spelling, or grammar— anything goes! This is for your eyes only.

3 Don't read what you are writing until the timer has sounded.

When you have finished, read what you have written. Don't judge it, but simply read it as practice. You may like to highlight particular words or phrases that stand out for you, or write a sentence or two in reflection.

I practice mindfulness meditation because ...

_____

_____

_____

_____

_____

_____

_____

_____

_____

_____

_____

_____

_____

_____

_____

_____

THE WAY FORWARD: SETTING INTENTIONS

An important part of the past few months has been exploring and connecting with our intention. We all need to have a reason to practice that acts as our guiding star. We might not always have it at the forefront of our mind, but we know what direction it encourages us to follow.

What practices have you found helpful (see page 186), and what would you like to continue with regularly?

What form would you like your formal practice to take in the future? Be as specific as you can about how frequently you intend to practice, the time and place, and what you intend to do.

To be reviewed on _____

(Choose a date between three and six weeks ahead when you can review and update your intention.)

ANY OTHER INTENTIONS?

Use the prompts below or create your own intentions. These can be open-ended, in the form of a "wish list," or you may find it helpful to set specific dates by which you'd like to do them, and tick the boxes when you're done. As always, be realistic, and if you don't manage to complete them in the intended time, don't be too hard on yourself.

[ ] Find a sitting group by _____

[ ] Explore retreat options: day by _____

residential by _____

[ ] Explore short courses by _____

Books I'd like to read:

_____ [ ]

_____ [ ]

_____ [ ]

_____ [ ]

_____ [ ]

_____ [ ]

_____ [ ]

_____ [ ]

CHECKLIST OF PRACTICES AND ACTIVITIES

Mark your preferred practices and activities—perhaps make a note of why or if there is a particular time when they are helpful. You can then revisit this list for ideas on mindful activities and practices to try.

PRACTICES
- ☐ Tuning into the Body
- ☐ Mindful Movement
- ☐ Mindful Eating
- ☐ Mindfulness of Breath and Body
- ☐ The Breathing Space
- ☐ Being With Sounds and Thoughts
- ☐ Being With the Difficult
- ☐ Self-compassion
- ☐ The Mountain

ACTIVITIES
- ☐ **WEEK 1:** Writing as Practice: Exploring Intention 1
- ☐ **WEEK 2:** The Importance of Reflecting
- ☐ **WEEK 3:** Cultivating the Attitudes
- ☐ **WEEK 4:** Savoring Our Experience
- ☐ **WEEK 5:** Breathing Through the Feet on the Floor
- ☐ **WEEK 6:** Exploring the Beam of Awareness
- ☐ **WEEK 7:** Exploring Felt Sensations
- ☐ **WEEK 8:** Seven ... Eleven
- ☐ **WEEK 9:** Sounds
- ☐ **WEEK 10:** Listening Mindfully
- ☐ **WEEK 11:** What Attitudes Are You Feeding?
- ☐ **WEEK 12:** Appreciating the Good
- ☐ **WEEK 13:** Experiencing the Unpleasant
- ☐ **WEEK 14:** Moving Out of Your Comfort Zone
- ☐ **WEEK 15:** Noticing the Narrative
- ☐ **WEEK 16:** Creating a Space

- [ ] **WEEK 17:** Writing as Practice: Exploring Intention 2
- [ ] **WEEK 18:** The Power of Attention
- [ ] **WEEK 19:** Being Present in Mind and Body
- [ ] **WEEK 20:** Seeing With Fresh Eyes
- [ ] **WEEK 21:** Ditch the Labels
- [ ] **WEEK 22:** Identifying Your Stress Triggers
- [ ] **WEEK 23:** The Power of Technology
- [ ] **WEEK 24:** Conversation as Practice
- [ ] **WEEK 25:** Exploring the Wanting Creature
- [ ] **WEEK 26:** Halfway Review
- [ ] **WEEK 27:** Exploring Resistance
- [ ] **WEEK 28:** Blue Sky Is Always There
- [ ] **WEEK 29:** What Does Acceptance Mean For Me?
- [ ] **WEEK 30:** Coping Space
- [ ] **WEEK 31:** Working with Impulses
- [ ] **WEEK 32:** Start From Where You Are
- [ ] **WEEK 33:** Taking a Mindful Minute
- [ ] **WEEK 34:** Exploring Alternate Viewpoints
- [ ] **WEEK 35:** Noticing the Judging Mind
- [ ] **WEEK 36:** Zoning Out
- [ ] **WEEK 37:** What Nourishes Me: An Action Plan
- [ ] **WEEK 38:** No One Else Has the Answer
- [ ] **WEEK 39:** Naming What Is Present
- [ ] **WEEK 40:** What Stops You Practicing?
- [ ] **WEEK 41:** A Typical Day
- [ ] **WEEK 42:** Taking Care of Ourselves
- [ ] **WEEK 43:** Practicing Kindness to Oneself
- [ ] **WEEK 44:** Being With Thoughts
- [ ] **WEEK 45:** No Man Is an Island
- [ ] **WEEK 46:** Making the Practice Your Own
- [ ] **WEEK 47:** Moving With Awareness
- [ ] **WEEK 48:** What Does Feeling Centered Feel Like?
- [ ] **WEEK 49:** Email as Practice
- [ ] **WEEK 50:** The Power of Silence
- [ ] **WEEK 51:** Writing as Practice: Exploring Intention 3
- [ ] **WEEK 52:** The Way Forward: Setting Intentions

FIND OUT MORE

ORGANIZATIONS

Centre for Mindfulness Research & Practice (CMRP)

Bangor, North Wales, UK

As well as professional trainings, the CMRP offers mindfulness teaching and retreats to the general public.

www.bangor.ac.uk/mindfulness

Oxford Mindfulness Centre, Oxford, UK

Offers professional training as well as mindfulness courses for the general public.

http://oxfordmindfulness.org

Be Mindful

The Mental Health Foundation's resource on mindfulness including UK teacher listings, information, and an online course.

http://bemindful.co.uk

Center for Mindfulness in Medicine, Health Care, and Society, Massachusetts, USA

Resources, professional trainings, and courses for the general public.

www.umassmed.edu/cfm

Sounds True

An excellent resource for purchasing audio cds and downloads on mindfulness and other topics around personal transformation.

www.soundstrue.com

BOOKS

Buddha's Brain: The Practical Neuroscience of Happiness, Love and Wisdom by Rick Hanson and Daniel J. Siegel (New Harbinger Publications, 2009)

Full Catastrophe Living (Revised Edition) by Jon Kabat-Zinn (Piatkus, 2013)

The Mindful Path to Self Compassion: Freeing Yourself from Destructive Thoughts and Emotions by Christopher Germer (The Guilford Press, 2009)

The Mindful Way Through Depression by Mark Williams, John Teasdale, Zindel Segal and Jon Kabat-Zinn (The Guilford Press, 2007)

Mindfulness: A Practical Guide to Finding Peace in a Frantic Work by Professor Mark Williams and Dr Danny Penman (Piatkus, 2011)

Mindfulness for Health: A Practical Guide for Relieving Pain, Reducing Stress and Restoring Well-being by Vidyamala Burch and Dr Danny Penman (Piatkus, 2013)

Mindfulness in Eight Weeks: The Revolutionary 8-week Plan to Clear Your Mind and Calm Your Life by Michael Chaskalson (Harper Thorsons, 2014)

Self Compassion by Kristin Neff (Hodder & Stoughton, 2011)

Wherever You Go There You Are: Mindfulness Meditation for Everyday Life by Jon Kabat-Zinn (Piatkus, 2004)

Other authors you may like to explore include Jack Kornfield, Sharon Salzberg, Joseph Goldstein, and Pema Chodron.

INDEX

ACKNOWLEDGMENTS

No book is ever produced in isolation and *A Year of Living Mindfully* is the product of a great team at CICO Books. As well as those behind the scenes, particular thanks are due to Cindy Richards for being so enthusiastic and supportive of the original idea, Dawn Bates for her gentle managing of the process, and Amy Louise Evans for her wonderful illustrations—despite the tight deadlines!

I'd also like to thank those who continue to support my mindfulness practice in so many ways particularly Eluned Gold, Melissa Blacker, and David Rynick.